INTRODUCING
Kafka

David Zane Mairowitz and Robert Crumb

NORTHAM.

PRESS

Introducing Kafka

Published by Kitchen Sink Press, Inc.,
320 Riverside Drive, Northampton, MA 01060.

Text © 1994 David Zane Mairowitz.
Illustrations © 1994 Robert Crumb.

Originally published as *Kafka for Beginners*
in 1993 by Icon Books Ltd., Cavendish House,
Cambridge Road, Barton, Cambridge.

First Kitchen Sink printing, May 1994

5 4 3

Kitchen Sink is a registered trademark
of Kitchen Sink Press, Inc.

Write for a free catalog of hundreds of
comics and related merchandise by
Robert Crumb and other artists,
or call 1-800-365-SINK.

Printed in the U.S.

ISBN 0-87816-282-8

"The image of a wide pork butcher's knife, swiftly and with mechanical regularity chopping into me, shaving off razor-thin slices which fly about due to the speed of the work."

Throughout most of his life, Franz Kafka imagined his own extinction by dozens of carefully elaborated methods. Those set down in his diaries, amongst mundane complaints of constipation or migraine, are often the most striking:

"To be dragged in through the ground-floor window of a house by a rope tied around my neck and then to be yanked upwards, bloody and mutilated, as if by someone not paying attention, with no consideration, through all the ceilings, furniture, walls and attics, until the last torn-off bits of me drop from the empty noose as it crashes through the tiles and comes to rest on the roof."

Kafka managed to turn this sometimes deliciously-evoked internal terror INSIDE-OUT — with himself torn and mutilated at its centre — as STORY-TELLING. He had no discernible World-View to share in his work, no guiding philosophy, only dazzling tales to deliver out of an extraordinarily acute subconscious. At best, an identifiable MOOD pervades his work, mysterious and difficult to pinpoint. Which has allowed the *"pork-butchers"* of modern culture to turn him into an ADJECTIVE.

No writer of our time, and probably none since Shakespeare, has been so widely over-interpreted and pigeon-holed. Jean-Paul Sartre claimed him for Existentialism, Camus saw him as an Absurdist, his life-long friend and editor, Max Brod, convinced several generations of scholars that his parables were part of an elaborate quest for an unreachable God.

Because his novels **THE TRIAL** and **THE CASTLE** deal with the inaccessibility of higher authority, *"Kafkaesque"* has come to be associated with the faceless bureaucratic infrastructure which the highly efficient Austro-Hungarian Empire bequeathed the Western world. In any case, it is an adjective that takes on almost mythic proportions in our time, irrevocably tied to fantasies of doom and gloom, ignoring the intricate Jewish Joke that weaves itself through the bulk of Kafka's work.

Before ever becoming the ADJECTIVE, Franz Kafka (1883-1924) was a Jew from Prague, born into its inescapable tradition of story-tellers and fantasists, ghetto-dwellers and eternal refugees. His Prague, *"a little mother"* with *"claws"*, was a place that suffocated him, but where he nonetheless chose to live all but the last eight months of his life.

Prague, at the time of Kafka's birth in 1883, was still part of the Hapsburg Empire in Bohemia, where numerous nationalities, languages and political and social orientations intermingled and coexisted, for better or worse. For someone like Kafka, a Czech-born German-speaker, who was really neither Czech nor German, forming a clear cultural identity was no easy matter.

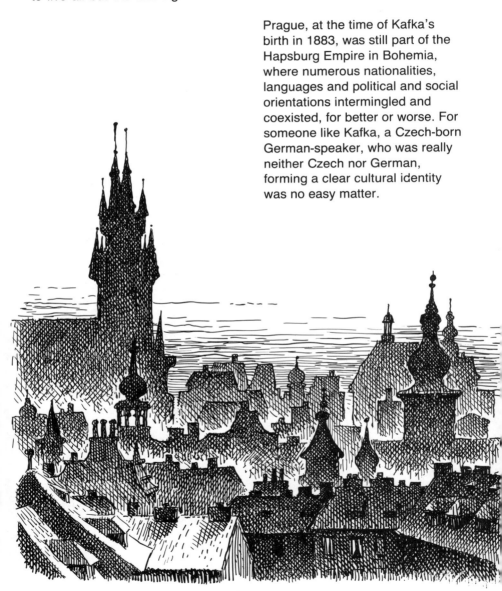

It goes without saying that for a Jew in this milieu, life was a delicate balancing act. You identified primarily with German culture, but lived among Czechs. You spoke German because it was close to Yiddish and was the Empire's official language. Czech nationalism was on the rise against German predominance, and the Germans generally treated the Czechs with contempt. And, of course, EVERYBODY hated the Jews.

Including, naturally, many *"assimilated"* Jews, who, like Kafka's father, didn't want to be reminded of their outsider status by their poorer cousins from Poland or Russia, the *"Ostjuden"*. Many better-off Jews would later become Zionists and learn Hebrew, rejecting Yiddish as a bastard language.

The Zionist Movement, founded in 1897 by Theodor Herzl, held that Jews, dispersed around the globe, should re-establish their homeland in Palestine. In the midst of numerous nationalist movements and rampant anti-Semitism, this early Zionism played an essentially protective role, to which many of Kafka's contemporaries were drawn.

These struggles inside the Jewish community were daily fare for the young Kafka, growing up in the middle of one of Europe's oldest ghettos.

"THIS NARROW CIRCLE ENCOMPASSES MY ENTIRE LIFE."

Kafka's "narrow circle", known as Josefov, wrapped itself around a complex of dark, meandering streets and alleyways (Judengassen) stretching from the edge of Prague's Old Town Square to the famous Charles Bridge on the Vltava (Moldau) river. In his youth, there were 6 synagogues in this crowded area, and beautiful Baroque buildings stared out onto rat-infested slums.

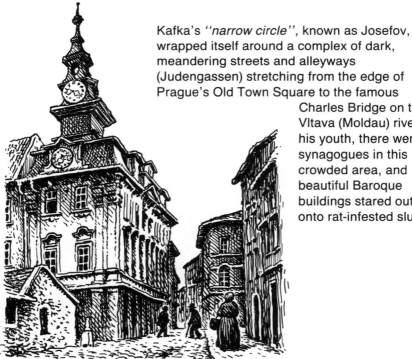

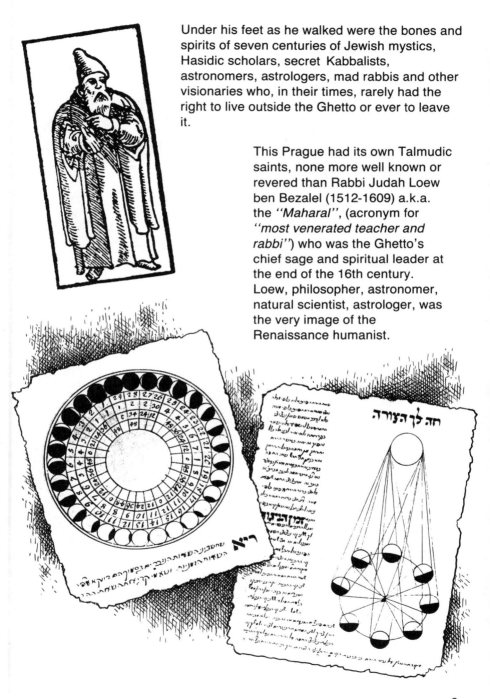

Under his feet as he walked were the bones and spirits of seven centuries of Jewish mystics, Hasidic scholars, secret Kabbalists, astronomers, astrologers, mad rabbis and other visionaries who, in their times, rarely had the right to live outside the Ghetto or ever to leave it.

This Prague had its own Talmudic saints, none more well known or revered than Rabbi Judah Loew ben Bezalel (1512-1609) a.k.a. the *"Maharal"*, (acronym for *"most venerated teacher and rabbi"*) who was the Ghetto's chief sage and spiritual leader at the end of the 16th century. Loew, philosopher, astronomer, natural scientist, astrologer, was the very image of the Renaissance humanist.

TITLE PAGE OF RABBI LOEW'S BOOK OF 1578

The Maharal held two contradictory principles, which he tried to reconcile: there was a *"horizontal"* or *"human"* power in the form of science, creativity, tolerance and doubt in confrontation with God's absolute *"vertical"* power, reducing man to dust and insignificance. Being a Jewish scholar, the questions he raised in regard to this contradiction could only lead to the raising of other questions, which is what Jewish Wisdom is all about.

It is also whispered that the Maharal played around with forbidden fruit, like the secret texts of the Kabbalah, which form the essence of Jewish mysticism, whose meanings are chiefly symbolic and only accessible (if at all) after years of scholarship. In the Kabbalah, the letters of the Hebrew alphabet were imbued with magic powers. According to the Kabbalistic expert, Gershom Scholem, such mystical impulses have all but vanished, *"but they still retain an enormous force in the books of Franz Kafka"*.

These forbidden scriptures figure in the most famous of all Prague legends, one firmly associated — rightly or wrongly — with Rabbi Loew . . .

Golem is, in effect, the Jewish Frankenstein monster, a heap of clay imbued with life by its creator, having immense power, but only able to use this power within prescribed limits. Legend has it that Rabbi Loew, in order to give life to the inert heap of clay, writes the Hebrew sign EMETH (truth) on its forehead.

Golem then becomes a kind of servant and protector of the Ghetto. But, of course, he's not allowed to work on the Sabbath, so the Rabbi, every Friday night, is forced to erase the first letter, Aleph, leaving Mem and Taw which, together in Hebrew, spell out METH (Death). Then, on the one Saturday when the Maharal has forgotten to erase the first letter . . .

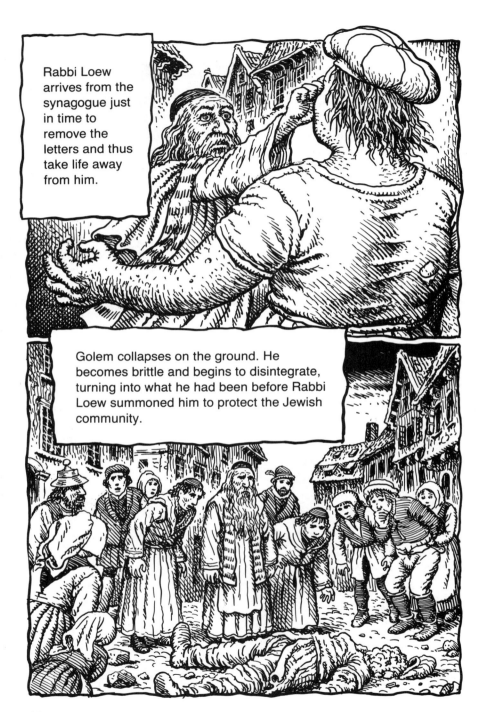

Rabbi Loew arrives from the synagogue just in time to remove the letters and thus take life away from him.

Golem collapses on the ground. He becomes brittle and begins to disintegrate, turning into what he had been before Rabbi Loew summoned him to protect the Jewish community.

14

To his son-in-law and to his pupil, with whom he had made the Golem, Loew says:

"Don't forget this event. Let it be a lesson to you. Even the most perfect Golem, risen to life to protect us, can easily change into a destructive force. Therefore let us treat carefully that which is strong, just as we bow kindly and patiently to that which is weak. Everything has its time and place."

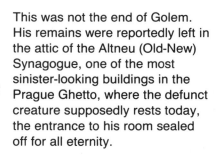

This was not the end of Golem. His remains were reportedly left in the attic of the Altneu (Old-New) Synagogue, one of the most sinister-looking buildings in the Prague Ghetto, where the defunct creature supposedly rests today, the entrance to his room sealed off for all eternity.

Never a practising or religious Jew, and rarely mentioning the Ghetto legends in his works, Kafka would have had no way of avoiding their fantastical imprint on the social memory of a Jewish boy in his time and place.

Yet, despite the ADJECTIVE's connotations, it wasn't Kafka who gave the Prague Ghetto its literary *"sinister"* reputation, but rather a non-resident, non-Jew named Gustav Meyrink. Meyrink's melodramatic, hack novel, **THE GOLEM** (1913), treats of murder and intrigue, dark musty alley-ways, and the Golem is a figure of terror who appears every 33 years. *"Lurking and waiting . . . waiting and lurking . . . the terrible perpetual motto of the Ghetto."*

But what Meyrink also recorded, and what Kafka himself grew up with, was the demolition of part of the Ghetto in 1906.

For Meyrink, the Prague Ghetto had been a *"demonic underworld, a place of anguish, a beggarly and phantasmagoric quarter whose eeriness seemed to have led to its demoralization"*.

Yet, once the *"sanitary"* clearance plan was under way, many of the poorer Jews refused to leave. As soon as the walls came tumbling down, they put up wire fences to replace them.

Kafka would later call the Ghetto *"my prison cell – my fortress"*.

When Hermann Kafka set up his fancy goods shop in 1882, it was on Celetna Street, just outside the Ghetto precinct. A self-made man, up from dire poverty, he took some pains to distance himself from the Jewish community, even officially declaring his family as Czech. This did not stop him from having his son bar-mitzvahed or from dragging the boy along on his token outings to the synagogue, two or three times a year.

For the boy Franz, these occasions were the *"preliminary sketches made in hell for later life in an office."*

Kafka's relation to his Jewish origins remained ambiguous, except towards the end of his life, when he seriously dreamed of escaping to Palestine. He certainly showed little sign, as some critics say he did, of any interest in Judaism as a religion (or in religion itself, for that matter). He did, however, show a strong intellectual interest in Hasidism.

The modern Hasidic movement was founded in Poland in the 18th Century by Baal-Shem-Tov, who called for a spiritual renaissance, not merely through prayer, but also through singing, dancing and ecstatic joy.

What excited Kafka, and surely had an impact on his stories, was the mystical, anti-rational side of Hasidism, where earthly reality was continuous with unearthly reality, where mystical value was to be found in the details of everyday life, and where God was everywhere and easily contactable.

R. ISRAEL BEN ELIEZER (CIRCA 1700-1760) BETTER KNOWN AS BAAL SHEM (HEALER) TOV, WAS BY PROFESSION A PEDDLER OF AMULETS.

Kafka's stories contain few overt references to Judaism, and whatever effect his immediate surroundings had on him, he seems to have mostly kept to himself. But the arrival in Prague of a small Yiddish Theatre troupe from Poland was to influence him strongly.

Prague's *"Westjuden"* didn't want to know from such overblown Schmalz (Jewish melodramatic sentimentality — literally *"grease"* or *"fat"*), a stark reminder of ghetto life, and mostly ignored the Yiddish actors. Kafka not only went to see them nearly every night, but began to study their traditions and take an interest in Yiddish as a language. And if he could see right through the chicken fat of their plots, he was nonetheless attracted to the fairy-tale aspect of the plays and stories.

No Jewish boy growing up in Prague at the turn-of-the-century could have been oblivious to the rabid hatred of Jews all around him.

God up in Heaven has it good
There are no Jews in His neighborhood.
But that means, for what it's worth,
There are more of them here on Earth.
So everyone who's brave and well-bred
Grab a club and smash their heads.
For only then will things be right
When not one Jew is left in sight.

To Jews were attributed every horror imaginable, including vampirism, all given sustenance by the existence of the *"mysterious"* Ghetto.

But no anti-Semitic myth was more prevalent in Eastern Europe at the time than that of . . .

The idea was that, in order to make their Matzos (unleavened flat bread, eaten primarily at Passover), Jews used Christian blood instead of water to bind the dough.

In April, 1899 (Kafka was 16), just around Passover, a nineteen-year-old Christian girl was found dead in Bohemia with her throat cut. Immediately the cry went up that she had been *"made kosher"* (literally *"fit for use"*, in compliance with Jewish dietary laws). A Jewish shoemaker, Leopold Hilsner, was denounced on no evidence and railroaded into a trial and death sentence, which was later commuted to life imprisonment. For Kafka, whose own grandfather had been a kosher butcher, the ritual murder outcry must have had resonance.

But more immediately, for him and his family, in the wake of the Hilsner case, came a wave of boycotts, accompanied by anti-Semitic riots and attacks on Jewish shops.

Franz Kafka was never one of those harassed or beaten up on the street because he was, or simply looked like, a Jew. Yet, however much he may have retired into himself and pushed these events out of direct reach, it would have been impossible, as for most Jews, to absent himself intellectually from the collective fate.

Like all assimilated Jews, one of the things he had to *"assimilate"* was a measure of "healthy anti-Semitism". Most Jews of that time (or any other) absorbed the daily menace of anti-Semitism and turned it inward against themselves. Kafka was no exception to feelings of Jewish Self-Hatred . . .

"WHAT DO I HAVE IN COMMON WITH THE JEWS? I DON'T EVEN HAVE ANY-THING IN COMMON WITH MYSELF!"

...WHICH, IN ITS HUMOROUS SELF-DEPRECATION, IS *EXACTLY* WHAT HE HAD IN COMMON WITH THE JEWS!

"SOMETIMES I'D LIKE TO STUFF ALL JEWS (MYSELF INCLUDED) IN-TO THE DRAWER OF A LAUNDRY BASKET...THEN OPEN IT TO SEE IF THEY'VE SUFFO-CATED."

But sooner or later, even the most hateful of Jewish Self-Hatreds has to turn around and laugh at itself. In Kafka, the duality of dark melancholy and hilarious self-abasement is nearly always at work. *"KAFKAESQUE"* is usually swollen with notions of terror and bitter anguish. But Kafka's stories, however grim, are nearly always also . . . FUNNY.

Those who knew Kafka well felt he lived behind a "glass wall". He was there, smiling, kindly, a good listener, a faithful friend and yet, somehow, inaccessible. A jumble of complexes and neuroses, he managed to give the impression of distance, grace, serenity and, at times, even SAINTLINESS.

Hermann Kafka (1852-1931)

His capacity for swallowing his fear of others and turning this against himself, rather than against its source is the stuff of all his work. Nowhere is this more apparent than in his relation to this man . . .

Kafka lived with his parents nearly all his life (even when he was financially independent and could have moved out), in very close quarters where his hyper-sensitivity to noise was put to the test on a daily basis. For Kafka Senior, a giant of a man, his son was a failure and a *Schlemiel* (good-for-nothing), a grave disappointment. He never hesitated to let him know.

And, at the dinner table . . .

Kafka's lifelong awe in the face of superior POWER, made famous in the novels **THE TRIAL** and **THE CASTLE,** begins with Hermann Kafka. He feared and hated his teachers at school, but had to see them as *"Respektspersonen"*, to be respected for no other reason than that they were in positions of authority.

But he never rebelled. Instead, he turned his fear into self-abasement or psychosomatic illness. In every contretemps with authority, he made himself the guilty party. Moreover, as in the classical relationship between master and slave, between colonizer and colonized, HE BEGAN TO SEE HIMSELF THROUGH HIS FATHER'S EYES.

THE Judgment

IN THIS EARLY STORY GEORG BENDEMANN, A YOUNG MERCHANT LIVING ALONE WITH HIS AGING FATHER SINCE THE DEATH OF HIS MOTHER, HAS BEEN WRITING TO AN OLD FRIEND IN RUSSIA.

I have saved my best news for the end. I've become engaged to Fräulein Frieda Brandenfeld, a girl from a well-to-do family.

WITH THE LETTER IN HIS POCKET, GEORG CROSSED THE CORRIDOR TO HIS FATHER'S ROOM...

GEORG REMOVED HIS FATHER'S WOOLLEN TROUSERS AND SOCKS, THEN PICKED HIM UP AND CARRIED HIM TO BED. SEEING THE NOT PARTICULARLY CLEAN STATE OF HIS FATHER'S UNDERWEAR, HE REPROACHED HIMSELF FOR HAVING NEGLECTED THE OLD MAN.

AN AWFUL FEELING CAME OVER HIM AS HE BECAME AWARE THAT HIS FATHER, CURLED UP IN HIS ARMS, WAS PLAYING WITH THE WATCH-CHAIN AT HIS LAPEL.

ONCE HE WAS IN BED, HOWEVER, EVERYTHING SEEMED TO BE FINE...

AM I COVERED UP NOW?

AM I COVERED UP?

SEE, YOU LIKE IT IN BED...

DON'T WORRY... YOU'RE WELL COVERED UP...

34

GEORG FELT HIMSELF THRUST FROM THE ROOM. HE TOOK THE STAIRS AT A RUSH... OUT THE DOOR HE SHOT, HIS MOMENTUM CARRYING HIM ACROSS THE ROAD TO THE WATER'S EDGE...

HE CLUTCHED THE RAILING AS A HUNGRY MAN WILL CLUTCH AT FOOD. HE VAULTED OVER IT, EXPERT GYMNAST THAT HE HAD BEEN IN HIS YOUTH, MUCH TO HIS PARENTS' PRIDE. STILL HOLDING ON WITH WEAKENING GRIP, HE GLIMPSED A BUS THROUGH THE BARS, KNEW IT WOULD EASILY COVER THE NOISE OF HIS FALL...

DEAR PARENTS, I DID LOVE YOU, ALWAYS...

CROSSING THE BRIDGE AT THAT MOMENT WAS A SIMPLY ENDLESS STREAM OF TRAFFIC.

35

This wasn't the only time Kafka would arrange to have himself SENTENCED TO DEATH. It had to be that way. Suicide wasn't in the cards.

But Death itself took too long. For Kafka, there would always be another way: making himself "DISAPPEAR".

There were many variants on this theme, although it would always be a matter of making himself SMALL. His existence, as such, was an offence against nature. He saw himself as an object, for example, a wooden clothes-rack, pushed into the middle of the room.

Or: "A picture of my existence . . . would show a useless wooden stake covered in snow . . . stuck loosely at a slant in the ground in a ploughed field on the edge of a vast open plain on a dark winter night."

If Kafka was alienated from his country, his surroundings, his family, he was also a stranger in his own body. SHAME walked with him from early on.

But he also lived the shame and inadequacy of the perceived Jewish stereotype: knock-kneed, weak-chested, cowardly, an emphasis on the intellect at the expense of the body. In his adult life, Kafka would follow dozens of ''hygienic'' programmes, diets, fitness courses, etc. to try and counter this image.

At the same time, he was fit enough to swim in the Moldau in winter, go for long, exhausting walks in the mountains, go horseback riding, etc. More contradictory still, his friends often described him as having a refined elegance, something of a dandy and even a Don Juan.

But the fixed idea was stronger than fact. His lack of physical self-confidence was imprinted in childhood and would remain with him to the end.

Certainly in the domain of SEX, with which he was never at ease, except perhaps in some of Prague's numerous bordellos.

What was there to do with this body which he saw as too thin, gangling, graceless, an offence to the eyes and, what's more, in everyone's way? It would have to be reduced, starve itself, go into hiding or simply transform itself into a beast, preferably one whose belly touched the ground and could scurry away without causing the world too much unpleasantness.

"As Gregor Samsa awoke one morning after disturbing dreams, he found himself transformed in his bed into an enormous bug."

This, very likely the most famous first sentence in modern literature, begins Kafka's masterpiece:

METAMORPHOSIS

FRANZ KAFKA

DIE VERWANDLUNG

"Als Gregor Samsa eines Morgens aus unruhigen Träumen erwachte, fand er sich in seinem Bett zu einem ungeheueren Ungeziefer verwandelt."

DER JÜNGSTE TAG * 22/23

KURT WOLFF VERLAG · LEIPZIG

1916

"HE WAS LYING ON HIS BACK, WHICH WAS HARD, AS IF MADE OF ARMOUR... HIS MANY LEGS...WAVED HELPLESSLY IN FRONT OF HIS EYES."

Samsa, a travelling salesman, was the family's provider. Because of him, his father had been able to retire, and his sister could expect to study the violin at the music conservatory.

I'M GETTING OUT OF BED NOW... JUST BE PATIENT...FUNNY HOW SOMETHING LIKE THIS CAN HIT YOU...

...HIS WORK RECENTLY HAS BEEN MOST UN-SATISFACTORY...

For this reason, the first person to witness his change, along with his family, was the Chief Clerk of his firm, who had arrived because Gregor, for the first time in his life, was late for work.

41

The transformation was not complete and never would be. Gregor had to remain conscious of the revulsion he induced in others. He spent his days listening to his family through the door of his room . . .

. . . or negotiating his new body around the room's furniture or learning new skills: "he especially liked to hang suspended from the ceiling; he could breathe easier; his body swayed lightly from side to side; and in the blissful state induced by hanging there it sometimes happened to his surprise that he let go and fell to the floor."

He found "a bowl of fresh milk with little bits of white bread floating in it". But "he didn't like it, although milk had been his favourite drink . . ."

Instead, his sister Grete left "a selection of food, laid out on an old piece of newspaper . . ."

42

THERE WERE OLD HALF-ROTTEN VEGE-TABLES; BONES FROM THE PREVIOUS EVEN-ING'S DINNER... A PIECE OF OLD CHEESE GREGOR WOULD HAVE CONSIDERED INEDIBLE TWO DAYS BEFORE...

GREGOR'S ONLY WISH WAS TO DO ALL HE COULD TO HELP HIS FAMILY FORGET THE DISASTER WHICH HAD PUT THEM INTO A STATE OF DESPERATION ... WHENEVER HE HEARD THEM MENTION THE NEED TO EARN MONEY HE FELT FULL OF SHAME AND GRIEF...

43

Gregor's world now altered perceptibly. His sight began to worsen, so that he no longer recognised the street outside his window which now *"looked out onto a deserted wasteland where grey sky and land blended into one another"*.

Most urgently, he had to spare his sister the sight of him: *". . . one day he dragged a sheet on his back to the sofa and hid himself completely in it."*

COME IN, MOTHER, HE'S OUT OF SIGHT...

Grete had the idea of removing all the room's furniture, which hindered Gregor's movements. She could not, however, do this on her own.

"They were removing all the things Gregor cherished . . . Looking up to the wall, he spied the picture of the lady in fur which he had cut out of a magazine and framed himself. He would allow no one to touch that."

"He darted from his hiding place, quickly crawled up to it and pressed himself to the glass. He clung to his picture and would not let it be taken away. He would rather jump on his sister's face." His mother now saw the "huge brown mass on the flowered wallpaper" and fell fainting on the couch.

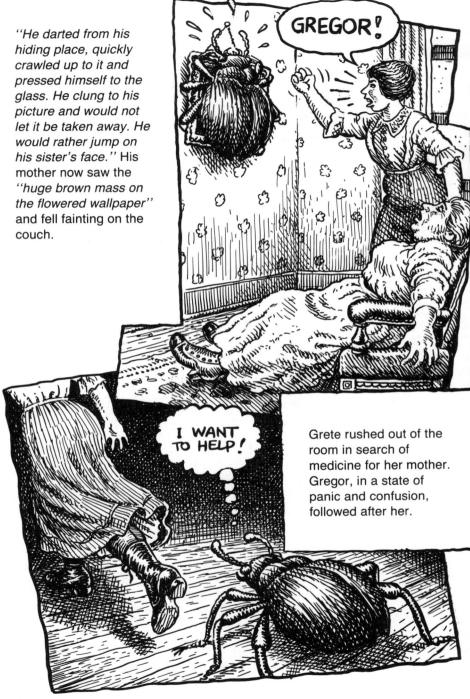

Grete rushed out of the room in search of medicine for her mother. Gregor, in a state of panic and confusion, followed after her.

Returning with several medications, his sister was startled by Gregor's presence in the living room, and dropped a bottle onto the floor. Gregor's face was cut by a splinter of glass and some of the corrosive substance splashed on him.

Running back to Gregor's room, Grete banged the door shut, leaving him stranded in the living room.

For a few minutes all was quiet, but then his father, who had been forced out of retirement to find a new job, came home. Gregor now had to attempt to placate him.

He crawled quickly to the door of his room and crouched against it to show that he was more than willing to go back in peacefully.

WHAT HAPPENED?

MOTHER'S FAINTED, BUT SHE'S ALL-RIGHT NOW.... GREGOR'S ESCAPED!

I KNEW IT! I KEPT TELLING YOU IT WOULD HAPPEN, BUT YOU WOMEN NEVER LISTEN!

His father, however, was in no mood to observe such niceties.

AH HA!

FROM THE FIRST DAY OF HIS NEW LIFE HIS FATHER BELIEVED THAT HE COULD ONLY BE DEALT WITH BY THE UTMOST SEVERITY.

THE LITTLE RED APPLES ROLLED OVER THE FLOOR AND BANGED INTO EACH OTHER. AN APPLE THROWN WITH HARDLY ANY STRENGTH GRAZED GREGOR'S BACK AND BOUNCED OFF HARMLESSLY. BUT ANOTHER ONE LANDED ON HIM AND SANK INTO HIS BACK.

"The pain was shocking, unbelievable. The last thing Gregor saw before he passed out was his mother rushing to his father, begging him to spare her son's life."

A month passed. Lamed from his injury, the apple festering in his back, Gregor was now *"covered in dust; hair and bits of old food stuck to his back and sides, and trailed after him . . ."* His once-beloved sister no longer bothered to clean his room.

With Gregor unable to support them, the family was forced to take in three lodgers. These upright gentlemen's penchant for order led to the storing of excess furniture and junk in Gregor's room.

One evening the lodgers asked Grete to play her violin for them.

Gregor, hearing the beautiful music, crawled into the room. *"Was he really an animal if music could move him so?"*

MY DEAR PARENTS! WE MUST GET RID OF THIS CREATURE! IT HAS TO GO! WE'VE TRIED OUR BEST TO LOOK AFTER IT. NO ONE CAN REPROACH US IN THE LEAST!

WE HAVE TO GET OVER THE IDEA THAT THIS IS GREGOR. IF THIS WERE GREGOR HE'D HAVE DISAPPEARED OF HIS OWN ACCORD... AS IT IS, THIS ANIMAL PERSECUTES US!

SHE'S RIGHT, BY GOD...

HE THOUGHT OF HIS FAMILY WITH TENDERNESS AND LOVE. EVEN MORE STRONGLY THAN HIS SISTER, HE CLUNG TO THE IDEA THAT HE MUST DISAPPEAR... HE REMAINED IN A STATE OF PEACEFUL MEDITATION UNTIL THE CHURCH CLOCK STRUCK THREE O'CLOCK. WITH THE FIRST RAYS OF DAWN OUTSIDE HIS WINDOW, HIS HEAD SANK TO THE FLOOR OF ITS OWN ACCORD AND THE LAST FLICKER OF BREATH ESCAPED HIS NOSTRILS.

In the morning, the charwoman found him.

IT'S CROAKED! THE THING'S CROAKED!

DON'T WORRY YOURSELVES ABOUT GETTING RID OF THAT THING...I'VE SEEN TO IT ALREADY...

Getting rid of *"the thing"*
breathed new life into the family.
They went for a tram ride in the
country. Nature's harmony had
been restored.

THE SAMSAS WERE SUDDENLY STRUCK BY THEIR DAUGHTER'S AWAKENING VIVACIOUSNESS... IN SPITE OF RECENT SORROW, SHE HAD BLOSSOMED INTO A PRETTY, WELL-BUILT GIRL.

AND, ALMOST AS IF CONFIRMING THEIR NEW VISION, AT THE END OF THE JOURNEY, THEIR DAUGHTER WAS THE FIRST TO SPRING TO HER FEET, STRETCHING HER YOUNG BODY...

Kafka did not want the insect to be seen. Concerning the cover of the first edition, he wrote to his publisher, Kurt Wolff: *"Not that, anything but that! The insect itself cannot be depicted. It mustn't even be shown from a distance."* This may have been his way of containing the horror of the transformation.

More likely, the line between his feelings about his body in human form and its "insecthood" was not all that clear.

It is also true that Gregor Samsa's metamorphosis is no miracle and is hardly even startling for the protagonist himself. It simply happens and he has no choice but to adapt. What counts most in this great fable is not so much Gregor's suffering, but rather that which he inadvertently inflicts on his parents and sister, mirroring Kafka's own feelings of inadequacy with regard to his family. (The description of the Samsa apartment resembles the Kafka flat in the Nikolasstrasse.)

He would never stop transforming himself into animals, his favourites being those which could crawl and quickly scamper away, although he had an inordinate terror of mice. Yet none of these "metamorphoses" ever has the repugnancy of Gregor Samsa's. Among Kafka's least-heralded talents is a great gift for writing animal stories and being able to do so from the creature's point of view.

Kafka would later change himself into a canine (**Investigations of a Dog**); an ape which has become more or less human (**Report to the Academy**); a singing mouse (**Josephine the Singer**), etc.

But perhaps the most extraordinary and acutely conscious of all his animals is the mole-like creature in the claustrophobic story . . .

THE BURROW

When he began to write seriously, Kafka fantasized his ideal workplace, cut off from the world: a sealed-off cellar where food would be brought to him and placed behind the farthest door. He would only have to move a short distance to collect it and eat it before resuming his creativity unhindered by human contact.
So it is with the ''I'' of **The Burrow** (**Der Bau**), one of Kafka's few first-person works. The creature has built itself a burrow with interlocking tunnels, heaps of meat in storage and a fortress-like stillness.

THE MOST WONDER-FUL THING ABOUT MY BURROW IS THE SILENCE. AT ANY MINUTE IT MAY BE BROKEN... BUT FOR NOW I CAN STROLL THROUGH ITS PASSAGES AND HEAR NOTHING EXCEPT THE STIRRING OF SOME TINY CREATURE WHICH I QUICKLY SILENCE WITH MY JAWS.

At the same time, there are unseen enemies in the burrow and Kafka's sense of impending terror is always there . . .

I'M NOT ONLY THREATENED BY OUTSIDE ENEMIES. THERE ARE ALSO ENEMIES IN THE EARTH'S ENTRAILS. I'VE NEVER SEEN THEM, BUT THEY'RE LEGENDARY AND I BELIEVE IN THEM...

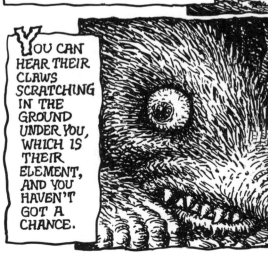

YOU CAN HEAR THEIR CLAWS SCRATCHING IN THE GROUND UNDER YOU, WHICH IS THEIR ELEMENT, AND YOU HAVEN'T GOT A CHANCE.

One such "enemy" seems to have tracked him down, and the "I" hears it in the walls and knows he is doomed. He will be trapped, torn to shreds (as usual) and no longer has the strength to resist, although, in the end, he cannot be sure that the beast is really aware of his presence.

58

In fact, Kafka would find dozens of ways to dispose of himself, right up until the end when tuberculosis was disposing of him and he most likely wanted, at last, to live.

No ordinary, run-of-the-mill hypochondriac, Kafka used ILLNESS, not merely as a metaphor for his troubled existence, but as yet another means of alienating himself from his family and, of course, from himself. In classical fashion, he localized his problem in that pipeline where food came and went, speaking of a rupture in *"the communication between stomach and mouth."* And when this seemingly Jewish ulcer behaved itself, the tension mounted upwards in unbearable headaches.

He also suffered from SLEEPLESSNESS, SHORTNESS OF BREATH, RHEUMATIC BACK PAIN, SKIN IRRITATION, was panicked by the idea of HAIR-LOSS or FAILING EYESIGHT or his SLIGHTLY DEFORMED TOE, and had such an over-sensitivity to noise that this led to near-permanent EXHAUSTION.

His lifelong response to his perceived illness came through various nature-cures and healing remedies, often to be found in the famous middle-European sanatoriums so prevalent at the time. Here he learned the Mueller body-building programme — calisthenics by an open window — which he practised for many years.

In many of the sanatoriums, nudism was the rule, but there was one exception:

Kafka — the kosher-butcher's grandson — also became a VEGETARIAN, claiming that meat made him feel like *"an alien and disgusting being in my bed."*

While his family ate Schnitzel and Sauerbraten, he ate mostly vegetables, nuts and fruit. And as if this wasn't enough to enrage Hermann Kafka, Franz also discovered the ideas of an American named Horace Fletcher, whose panacea for all illness was MASTICATION. Every bite of food had to be chewed more than 10 times.

There is also an argument to be made for Kafka's Jewish SELF-ABASEMENT contributing to both his lack of self-confidence and his unhappy body. In fact, at the time of the awakening Zionist consciousness around him, promoted by some of his closest friends, including Max Brod, Kafka took an active interest in the new physical clarion call. In 1912, the Zionist magazine, **Selbstwehr,** (which Kafka avidly read) railed against *"we Jews with out insistence on intellectual matters . . . our excess of nervousness and our physical weakness . . . all remnants of the ghetto."*

"In the age of racial hygiene and eugenics, the body must not be neglected because of the intellect! What makes a man is neither his mouth, nor his brain, nor his morality, but his DISCIPLINE! We demand JEWISH MANLINESS!"

ŞA-Dienſt erzieht zur Kameradſchaft Fähigkeit Kraft!

Which, of course, did not sound all that far off from other, more sinister "discipline and manliness" groups.

ILLNESS alone was not to pull Kafka free from the bruising psychic weight of his father. From 1912 on past the First World War, he toyed with another possible *"escape"* route, believing for a time that he might actually like to get MARRIED and raise a family of his own.

"A MAN WITHOUT A WIFE IS NOT A MAN."

TALMUD

The first — and longest — victim of this delusion was Felice Bauer (1887-1960), to whom Kafka was twice engaged — and twice disengaged — in the years from 1912-1917. He first wrote of her: *"Bony, empty face that clearly showed its emptiness."*
He only needed to see Felice once, and then only for a few hours, before he decided to *"win"* her over — Kafka style.

64

That she became the blank wall on which he alternately scribbled and effaced the graffiti of his fixed marriage idea is evident in the extraordinary body of letters written to her, forming a literary document as dense and alert as any novel he subsequently wrote.

In his lifetime, he had important relationships with four women, three of them — Felice Bauer, Grete Bloch and Milena Jesenska — almost exclusively by letter. *"Letter writing,"* he would later claim, *"is an intercourse with ghosts, not only with the ghost of the receiver, but with one's own, which emerges between the lines of the letter being written . . . Written kisses never reach their destination, but are drunk en route by these ghosts."*

Felice lived and worked in Berlin and, although the distance from Prague was a mere six hours by train, the kilometers were sufficient protection for Kafka. It is perfectly clear that, had she lived in Prague, there would have been no relationship.

In any case, from the second letter on, he begins describing his *"illnesses"* and providing her with a thousand examples of his unworthiness, thereby planning his withdrawal even while wooing her.

"AFTER ALL, YOU ARE A GIRL, AND YOU WANT A MAN, NOT AN EARTHWORM."

In the five years of their correspondence, they actually saw each other for a time totalling not more than several weeks. Once, when they were together, his watch had been running an hour and a half fast for three months, and that had made him happy. Now, to his distress, she was setting it *"right"*.

They also seem to have performed the *"disease of the instincts"* on one of their rare meetings, and it does not appear to have provoked in Kafka the desire for more. By August 1917, after five years of trying to save himself from his father by marrying, he now needed to save himself from marriage. A random, disconnected diary entry from this time reads:

"NO, LEAVE ME ALONE! NO, LEAVE ME ALONE," I SHOUTED ENDLESSLY ALL ALONG THE STREETS, WHILE AGAIN AND AGAIN SHE GRABBED AT ME, AGAIN AND AGAIN THE SIREN'S CLAWED HANDS STRUCK SIDEWAYS OR OVER MY SHOULDERS AT MY BREAST."

Some days after this, the *"siren's claws"* must have reached their mark. Kafka was too cowardly to tell Felice that it was over for good, but a sudden haemorrhaging of the lungs — the first sign of the tuberculosis that would kill him seven years later — did the job for him.

When it became clear to Kafka that he was CONDEMNED TO WRITE, *"everything hurried in that direction,"* while everything that smacked of *"sex, eating, drinking, philosophy, above all, music . . . atrophied . . ."* in him. Writing, for him, was both an escape from, and revenge against, his father. But, of course, it was more — and less — than that:

"I HAD GOT SOME DISTANCE AWAY FROM YOU, THROUGH MY OWN EFFORTS, ALTHOUGH IT WAS A BIT LIKE THE WORM WHO BREAKS AWAY WITH ITS FRONT PART WHEN SOMEONE STEPS ON ITS TAIL END."

THE EARTHWORM AGAIN

"ALL MY WRITING IS ABOUT YOU."

UHH... PUT IT ON MY BEDSIDE TABLE...

WITH DEDICATION: "TO MY FATHER"

For a businessman like Hermann Kafka, there was no greater waste of time than his son's scribbling. But for Kafka too, there was never the slightest question of this becoming his PROFESSION. He did not want to earn money by writing. He studied law at Prague's Charles University, which prepared him essentially for a bureaucratic post, becoming *"Herr Doktor Kafka"*. And soon after, he was given a position in which he would remain until nearly the end of his life.

His job for the **Workman's Accident Insurance Institute for the Kingdom of Bohemia in Prague**, where he was one of two token Jews in a company with closed hiring practices, was both a nightmare and a blessing. On the one hand, it took valuable time away from his writing. But it also gave him a steady income and a measure of self-respect and, in his decision-making capacity, he was able to contribute to reducing the rate of industrial accidents in Bohemia.

Industrial workers had traditionally been subject to ghastly workplace accidents. In the area of Kafka's jurisdiction . . .

...."PEOPLE FALL DRUNKENLY FROM SCAFFOLDING INTO MACHINES, BEAMS COLLAPSE... LADDERS COME CRASHING TO THE GROUND, WHATEVER IS LIFTED UP FALLS DOWN, WHATEVER IS SPREAD ON THE GROUND PEOPLE TRIP OVER, AND IT GIVES ONE A HEADACHE TO THINK OF ALL THOSE YOUNG GIRLS IN CHINAWARE FACTORIES WHO KEEP FALLING DOWN STAIRS WITH HUGE PILES OF DISHES IN THEIR ARMS."

Kafka's time at the Institute coincided with a new emphasis on safety, as a complement to insurance benefit. He himself, instinctively siding with the underdog, oversaw the implementation of many such measures, and was personally responsible for saving hundreds of lives, primarily in the lumber industry.

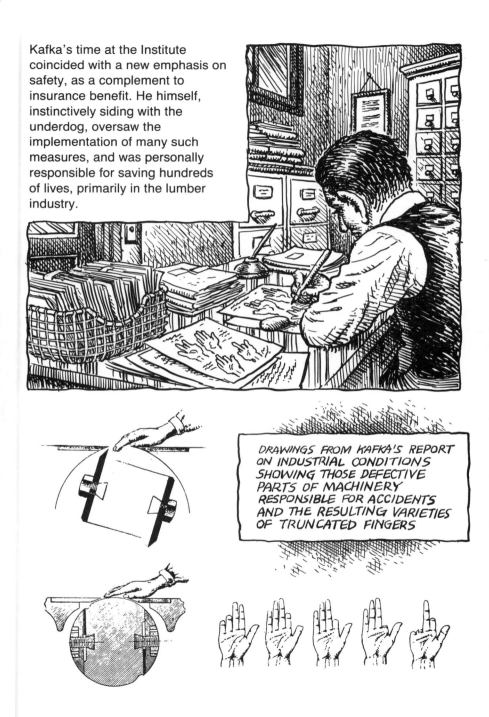

DRAWINGS FROM KAFKA'S REPORT ON INDUSTRIAL CONDITIONS SHOWING THOSE DEFECTIVE PARTS OF MACHINERY RESPONSIBLE FOR ACCIDENTS AND THE RESULTING VARIETIES OF TRUNCATED FINGERS

His job was also a way of placating his father, who would now have to find other reasons for treating his son as a good-for-nothing.

Working by day would mean writing at night in the cramped apartment, where he still lived with his parents and three sisters. This was hardly conducive to concentration ...

The only solution was a kind of self-hypnosis or *"interior emigration"* which simultaneously cut him off from the world and allowed him to take it all in . . .

"WRITING...IS A DEEPER SLEEP THAN DEATH... JUST AS ONE WOULDN'T PULL A CORPSE FROM ITS GRAVE, I CAN'T BE DRAGGED FROM MY DESK AT NIGHT."

"Every word first looks around in every direction before letting itself be written down by me."

It's 1914. If Hermann Kafka is still a background cause of his son's feverish nocturnal writing, it has gone far beyond the banality of their ongoing Oedipal war, and there are other important influences at work. Kafka is writing about POWER. And Submission. And Humiliation. The superior POWER that makes its object want to, as we have seen, reduce itself to something smaller that can scurry away on its little belly.

At the same time, events are shaping themselves around him which will set the 20th Century on its Horror Course. As with everything else, Kafka can tell the time before the clock strikes.

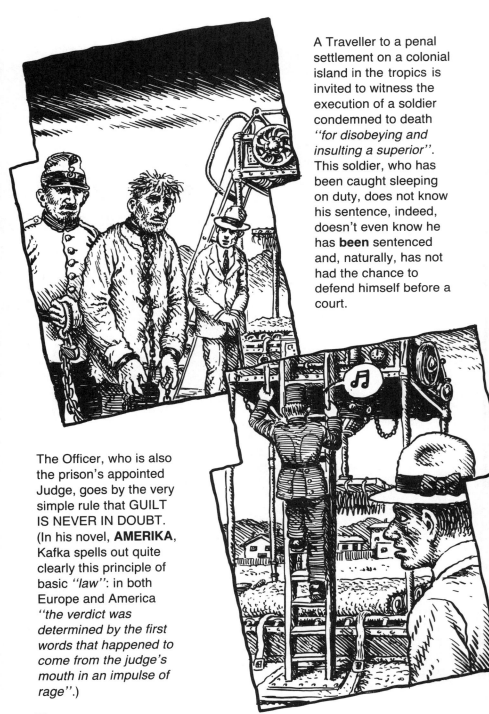

A Traveller to a penal settlement on a colonial island in the tropics is invited to witness the execution of a soldier condemned to death *"for disobeying and insulting a superior"*. This soldier, who has been caught sleeping on duty, does not know his sentence, indeed, doesn't even know he has **been** sentenced and, naturally, has not had the chance to defend himself before a court.

The Officer, who is also the prison's appointed Judge, goes by the very simple rule that GUILT IS NEVER IN DOUBT. (In his novel, **AMERIKA**, Kafka spells out quite clearly this principle of basic *"law"*: in both Europe and America *"the verdict was determined by the first words that happened to come from the judge's mouth in an impulse of rage"*.)

This procedure — or lack of one — is also at work in **THE TRIAL**, except that the victim, Joseph K., will question and protest against it. In the **Penal Colony**, Kafka is still sending bemused lambs to the slaughter: *"the condemned man looked like such a submissive little dog that he might have been left to wander the surrounding hills and only whistled for at the moment of execution"*.

79

The Officer, knowing that this form of capital punishment was no longer in favour, sought the approval and aid of the Traveller. He urged him to speak up on behalf of the machine.

Taking a paper from a small leather wallet, the Officer held it up for the Traveller to look at.

After carefully setting the paper in the designer, the Officer quickly began removing his clothes . . . . The Traveller knew what was going to happen, but felt he had no right to interfere in any way.

AS SOON AS HE FINISHED TAKING OFF A GARMENT, HE FLUNG IT INTO THE PIT WITH AN IMPATIENT JERK.

The Officer climbed naked onto the "bed", and allowed himself to be strapped down by the condemned man and the soldier, even accepting the stub of felt in his mouth.

But something went wrong.

THE MACHINE WAS OBVIOUSLY DISINTE-GRATING...ITS EASY FUNCTIONING WAS AN ILLUSION...INSTEAD OF WRITING, THE HARROW WAS ONLY JABBING, AND THE BED, NOT TURNING THE BODY OVER, SIMPLY RAISING IT UP, QUIVERING, AGAINST THE NEEDLES...

...AND NOW THE LAST THING WENT WRONG AS WELL: THE BODY FAILED TO COME LOOSE FROM THE LONG NEEDLES BUT HUNG SUSPENDED ABOVE THE PIT WITHOUT FALLING...

HIS FACE REMAINED AS IN LIFE... WHAT THE OTHERS HAD FOUND IN THE MACHINE THE OFFICER HAD NOT FOUND... HIS LIPS WERE PRESSED TOGETHER, THE EYES OPEN, CALM AND FULL OF CONVICTION, THROUGH THE FOREHEAD CAME THE POINT OF THE BIG IRON SPIKE.

War was now breaking out all around him and the Hapsburg Empire would not survive its ultimate defeat four years later. All of the pent-up hatred between nationalities came to a head, and Kafka's Prague would never be the same again. From his window he watched a parade, *"organized by Jewish businessmen, who are German one day, Czech the next."*

LONG LIVE OUR BELOVED EMPEROR!!

At the same time, Czech nationalism was on the rise, its leaders seeing in the War a chance to escape the repressive claws of the Empire. As usual, the Jews were caught in the middle. The Czech nationalists were traditionally anti-Semitic, and they associated the Jews — primarily German-speaking — with the Hapsburgs.

Kafka himself never publicly took sides, and had only "hatred for the fighters, whom I passionately wish the worst." (Although he later apparently toyed with the idea of enlisting as a means of escaping his impending marriage!) But most Prague Jews supported the Germans against the Allies (England, France, Japan, Russia, Belgium, Serbia and Montenegro), an irony of history which, only a decade later, would backfire in their faces.

In the midst of these events, Kafka sat down one night and wrote what is perhaps the **second** most memorable first line in modern literature:
"Someone must have been telling lies about Josef K., for without having done anything wrong he was arrested one morning."

Begun in 1914, this is probably his most well-known book, and certainly provides the basis for the popular notion of *"Kafkaesque"*. What the story demonstrates most clearly about Kafka-the-Night-Writer is the precision, humour and lack of overt emotion with which he can describe all his own nightmares.

THE TRIAL

DER PROZESS IN GERMAN, MEANING BOTH "TRIAL" AND "PROCESS"

From now on he will be *"K.,"* and he will wake up to find strange men milling about the boarding house where he lives, just as Gregor Samsa wakes up, setting **The Metamorphosis** in motion.

WHO **ARE** YOU?

YOU'VE BEEN ARRESTED...

SO IT SEEMS... BUT WHY?

I'M NOT PER-MITTED TO TELL YOU...PROCEED-INGS AGAINST YOU HAVE BEGUN AND YOU WILL BE TOLD EVERY-THING IN DUE COURSE...

No, he won't. Like Gregor Samsa, all Josef K. can do is learn to cope with his situation. With the difference that he does not simply accept his fate, but tries to understand it, and goes to any length to gather information about his case. In the end, he is no wiser, but he gets to be told a parable by a priest (who might as well be a Talmudic Rabbi) working for the court.

BEFORE THE LAW STANDS A DOOR-KEEPER...A MAN FROM THE COUNTRY ARRIVES AND ASKS TO BE ADMITTED TO THE LAW...THE DOOR-KEEPER SAYS HE CANNOT LET HIM IN NOW...THE MAN THEN ASKS IF HE'LL BE ALLOWED IN LATER...

POSSIBLY, BUT NOT NOW...

GO ON! TRY TO GET IN WITHOUT MY PERMISSION! BUT I TELL YOU, I'M ONLY THE LOWEST DOOR-KEEPER! IN EVERY HALL THERE'S ANOTHER ONE, MORE POWERFUL THAN THE LAST!

HE SITS THERE, DAY AFTER DAY, YEAR AFTER YEAR...

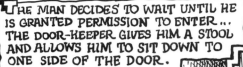

THE MAN FROM THE COUNTRY, HAVING BROUGHT MANY USEFUL THINGS ALONG, TRIES TO BRIBE THE DOOR-KEEPER, WHO ACCEPTS THEM ALL.

DURING ALL THESE MANY YEARS, THE MAN OBSERVES THE DOOR-KEEPER NEARLY ALL THE TIME. SO MUCH SO, THAT WHEN HE GETS OLD, HE KNOWS EVEN THE FLEAS ON HIS FUR COLLAR...

I'M ONLY TAKING THIS SO YOU WON'T FEEL YOU'VE LEFT SOMETHING UNTRIED...

PLEASE, PLEASE HELP ME...WON'T YOU ASK HIM TO LET ME IN ??

90

IN THE END HIS EYES GROW DIM, BUT HE PERCEIVES IN THE DARKNESS A RADIANT LIGHT COMING FROM INSIDE THE DOOR OF THE LAW.

HE IS NOT GOING TO LIVE MUCH LONGER NOW... HE BECKONS TO THE DOOR-KEEPER...

WHAT DO YOU WANT TO KNOW *NOW*??

EVERYONE HAS NEED OF THE LAW... SO WHY IS IT THAT IN ALL THESE YEARS NO ONE BUT MYSELF HAS ASKED TO ENTER ??

NO ONE ELSE *COULD* ENTER HERE, BECAUSE THIS DOOR WAS MEANT ONLY FOR YOU.

I'LL GO AND CLOSE IT NOW...

91

On the evening when Josef K's executioners come for him, he no longer protests or even tries to understand. Kafka spares us all heroics:

K. WALKED RIG-IDLY BETWEEN THEM, AND THE THREE OF THEM TOGETHER FORMED A SINGLE ENTITY. IT WAS AN ENTI-TY WHICH MIGHT ONLY BE FORMED OF LIFELESSNESS.

THEY WERE SOON AT THE EDGE OF TOWN, WHICH LED STRAIGHT INTO THE FIELDS, WHERE THEY CAME TO A SMALL DESERTED QUARRY...

THE TWO MEN LAID K. DOWN AND PILLOWED HIS HEAD AGAINST A LOOSE PIECE OF ROCK.

THEN ONE OF THE MEN REACHED INTO HIS FROCK COAT AND PULLED OUT A LONG THIN BUTCHERKNIFE, HELD IT UP AND EXAMINED IT IN THE MOONLIGHT.

ONE OF THEM HANDED THE KNIFE ACROSS K. TO THE OTHER, WHO THEN HANDED IT BACK ACROSS HIM.

K. KNEW PERFECTLY WELL THAT HE WAS MEANT TO TAKE THE KNIFE AND PLUNGE IT INTO HIMSELF, BUT HE DID NOT DO SO. INSTEAD HE TURNED HIS NECK AND LOOKED ABOUT HIM TO THE TOP OF THE HOUSE OPPOSITE THE QUARRY...

JUST AT THAT MOMENT A WINDOW FLEW OPEN THERE, AND A HUMAN SIL-HOUETTE, INDISTINCT TO HIM, SUDDENLY LEANED A LONG WAY OUT AND STRETCHED ITS ARMS OUT STILL FURTHER.

WHO WAS IT?? A FRIEND? SOMEONE WHO CARED? SOME-ONE WHO WANTED TO HELP? WAS HELP STILL POSSIBLE? WERE THERE OB-JECTIONS THAT HAD NOT BEEN VOICED? SURELY THERE WERE...

WHERE WAS THE JUDGE HE HAD NEVER SEEN? WHERE WAS THE HIGH COURT HE HAD NEVER REACHED? RAIS-ING HIS HANDS, HE SPREAD OUT ALL HIS FINGERS.

When Kafka read passages from **THE TRIAL** out loud to his friends, he is reported to have laughed uncontrollably.

When the War ended in 1918, much of the world Kafka had grown up in had been changed forever or simply swept away with the collapse of the Empire. Those the fighting hadn't killed were finished off by the Spanish flu, the 20th Century's answer to the Black Plague, which claimed some 20 million victims, most of them young and in apparent good health. Kafka's condition may have been weakened even further in this viral atmosphere.

Prague itself had changed in a very specific way, now no longer a part of the Kingdom of Bohemia, but rather of the new REPUBLIC OF CZECHOSLOVAKIA, where Czech nationalists could finally hit back with a vengeance. The hated Bohemian Germans no longer formed the dominant class, from which vantage point they had run the country's bureaucracy and saw to it that the bulk of the Czech working population was kept below German standards. And, inevitably, the German language became a victim of the new order of things. One day, when Kafka went to the office ...

German-speaking Czechs were summarily dismissed from their jobs, but Kafka, who could speak Czech and had never associated himself with one side or the other was, exceptionally, spared.

Germans were now assaulted in the street and their shops looted. And of course, for the Czechs, what better *"Germans"* to avenge themselves on than the Jews?

In November, a mob ran riot for three days, breaking into the German National Theatre and the Jewish Town Hall, where they destroyed the archives. As if a preview of things to come, they burned ancient Hebrew manuscripts before the Altneu Synagogue, right under the nose of the Golem, as it were. The new Czech mayor called this a *"demonstration of national consciousness"*.

Kafka was there.

I've been in the streets all afternoon bathing in Jew-hatred. People are calling them a "mangy race"... Isn't it only natural to leave? Staying here is like playing the heroic cockroach who refuses to be driven from the bathroom.. I looked out the window just now. Mounted police are getting ready for a charge, screaming crowds running in all directions...

In those years, over six thousand Jews left the country for Palestine. Kafka himself flirted with the idea until the end of his life.

99

He was on the slow road to DEATH. But he made one vital stop along the way . . .

She called him FRANK.

WERFEL

BROD

Milena Jesenska (1896-1944) met Kafka in 1919, when his work was known primarily by the intellectual groups that hung around the Café Arco in Prague.

One of the continent's most famous literary salons, the Arco counted Kafka amongst its *Stammgäste* (habitués), although he thought of himself more as an observer to the scene. It was here that bilingual writers like Franz Werfel and Max Brod tried to find some common ground between Czech and German, and where avant-garde literature from all over Europe could be read.

One of the "regulars" at the Arco was the highly promiscuous intellectual, Ernst Polack, whose young wife, Milena, was introduced fleetingly to Kafka, although he could scarcely remember the event.

Years later she became his Czech translator and his first-ever *Shiksa* (non-Jewish girlfriend), one of the very few Gentiles ever to play a significant role in his life. Born when Kafka himself was 13, he considered that her birth had been a Bar-Mitzvah present for him.

And, as far as such things can be judged, she was probably the only woman he ever really loved. You can smell it in the correspondence. The **Letters to Milena** are not like those to Felice, great literature parading as love, with a Jewish Pygmalion carving his wife out of stone.

Of course the old convoluted, labyrinthine self-doubt is still there. In a diary entry from 1922, he notes . . .

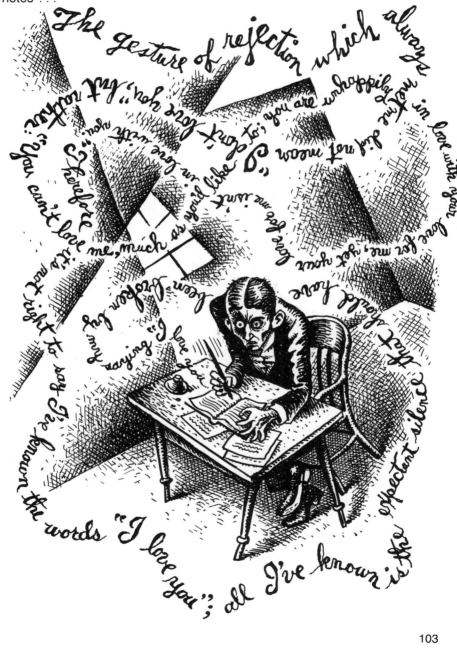

Yet, on the whole, the Milena letters are straightforward, with less of the usual ambiguity and self-abuse. Most of all, you get the feeling she has made him aware of his own longing and that he really WANTS her . . .

"*Since I love you...I love the whole world which includes your left shoulder -- no, first the right one (be so good as to pull your blouse out of the way)....and your face above me in the forest with me resting on your nearly naked breast.*"

When he told her . . .

"I'M DIRTY, MILENA, INFINITELY DIRTY, THAT'S WHY I'M OBSESSED WITH CLEANLINESS. NO SONG IS PURER THAN THAT SUNG IN THE DEPTHS OF HELL . . . "

She replied . . .

"I DON'T SEE ANYTHING DIRTY, NOTHING OF THE KIND, WHICH PROVOKES FROM OUTSIDE, ONLY EVERYTHING PRODUCING LIFE FROM INSIDE."

Milena was herself a writer and journalist, and something of an early feminist. If Kafka had viewed women as vampires or Valkyries before, representing for him all the collected dirt of the hated sex-act, here was one who forced him to face real feminine potential and made him confront his own fears.

When she suggested that they emerge flesh and blood out of their letters in order to meet in Vienna, he panicked as usual and piled up excuses for not coming. Her response to this was to ask him if he was Jewish.

Once again, Kafka was convinced that *"we will never live together, share the same apartment, body to body, be at the same table, never, not even in the same town . . ."*; but, *". . . instead of living together, we'll at least be able to lie down happily next to one another in order to die."*

Whatever degree of Kafka's dreaded *"disease of the instincts"* they may have engaged in (or not), Milena herself referred to it as *"men's business . . . that half-hour in bed"*.

And, in this respect, she seemed to know him better than anyone else.

"I KNEW HIS FEAR BEFORE I KNEW HIM ... IN THE FOUR DAYS FRANK WAS NEAR ME, HE LOST IT. WE EVEN LAUGHED ABOUT IT. BUT... HE WILL NEVER BE HEALTHY AS LONG AS HE HAS THIS FEAR... IT ISN'T JUST ABOUT ME, BUT ABOUT EVERYTHING WHICH IS SHAMELESSLY ALIVE, FOR EXAMPLE, THE FLESH. FLESH IS TOO OPEN, TOO NAKED : HE CAN'T BEAR THE SIGHT OF IT.... WHEN HE FELT THE FEAR COMING ON, HE WOULD STARE INTO MY EYES, WE WOULD WAIT FOR AWHILE... AND IT WOULD SOON PASS... EVERYTHING WAS SIMPLE AND CLEAR..."

" I DRAGGED HIM OVER THE HILLS BEHIND VIENNA, AND I RAN AHEAD BECAUSE HE WALKED SO SLOWLY, TRAMPING AFTER ME....IF I SHUT MY EYES I CAN *STILL* SEE HIS WHITE SHIRT AND SUN-TANNED NECK AND HIM EXERTING HIMSELF. HE WALKED UP AND DOWN ALL DAY, IN THE SUN, DIDN'T COUGH EVEN ONCE, ATE AND SLEPT WELL. HE WAS *SIMPLY* HEALTHY, AND IT SEEMED TO US THEN THAT HIS ILLNESS WAS NO MORE THAN A MERE COLD. "

Whatever her effect on him, there is a case to be made for Milena being the model for the character of Frieda in Kafka's great unfinished novel . . .

THE CASTLE
(DAS SCHLOSS, 1922)

IT WAS LATE EVENING WHEN K. ARRIVED. THE VILLAGE LAY DEEP IN SNOW. THE CASTLE HILL WAS HIDDEN IN DARKNESS AND FOG, AND NOT EVEN THE MEREST GLIMMER OF LIGHT INDICATED THE PRESENCE OF A CASTLE. K. STOOD FOR A LONG TIME ON THE WOODEN BRIDGE LEADING FROM THE MAIN ROAD INTO THE VILLAGE, GAZING AT THE SEEMING EMPTINESS ABOVE HIM.

THE CASTLE has been interpreted to death, the critical commentary on this one novel alone running into hundreds of volumes in dozens of languages. This is, in some measure, because it is unfinished, and therefore open territory for reading Kafka's intentions.

But the first paragraph shows that he has embarked on a fairy tale (Kafka read and loved fairy tales all his life) which will be labyrinthine. The Land Surveyor *"K."* (not even *"Josef K."*, just plain *"K"*) like the classical *"wanderer"*, has apparently been summoned to the village by the all-powerful authority from The Castle, the never-seen Count West-West. It is clear from the start that he will never get to the Castle, and that the usual rigid hierarchy of power will suppress his attempts.

THE NEXT MORNING...

WHEN K. FINALLY SEES THE CASTLE "HE WAS DISAPPOINTED... IT WAS NEITHER AN OLD FORTRESS NOR A NEW MANSION, BUT A DISMAL COLLECTION OF INNUMERABLE SMALL BUILDINGS PACKED TOGETHER. SWARMS OF CROWS CIRCLED AROUND THE ONLY TOWER..."

Most of the officials who work for the Castle are as aloof as the Count, and the villagers themselves are kept at a distance. K meets the local schoolmaster.

YOU KNOW THE COUNT, OF COURSE...?

NO...

WHAT?!? YOU DON'T KNOW THE COUNT??

WHY SHOULD I ?

S'IL VOUS PLAÎT, SOUVENEZ-VOUS, QU'IL Y A DES ENFANTS INNOCENTS PRESENTS!*

* PLEASE REMEMBER, THERE ARE INNOCENT CHILDREN PRESENT!

MIGHT I COME TO VISIT YOU ONE DAY, SIR? I'LL BE STAYING HERE FOR SOME TIME AND ALREADY FEEL A BIT LONESOME... I DON'T FIT IN WITH THE PEASANTS NOR, I IMAGINE, WITH THE CASTLE...

THERE IS NO DIFFERENCE BETWEEN THE PEASANTS AND THE CASTLE!

Although K's presence in the village appears to have stemmed from some bureaucratic confusion about the need for a Land Surveyor — a request going back a long time and apparently rescinded — the Castle sends him two *"assistants"*, Arthur and Jeremiah, two mad fools, Tweedledee and Tweedledum, straight out of the Yiddish theatre.

AT THE DOOR OF THE INN...

WHO *ARE* YOU? YOUR ASSISTANTS...

WHAT!? MY OLD ASSISTANTS I TOLD TO FOLLOW ME HERE AND WHOM I'M EXPECTING??

YES!

WELL, YOU'RE *LATE*...WHERE'S THE APPARATUS I GAVE YOU?

WE DON'T HAVE IT...

OH! THAT'S JUST FINE! DO YOU KNOW ANYTHING ABOUT SURVEYING??

NO...

BUT IF YOU ARE MY *OLD* ASSISTANTS, YOU MUST KNOW *SOMETHING* ABOUT SURVEYING !?!

WELL.... COME IN ....

Unable to find decent lodgings, exhausted and in need of sleep, K is led to another inn by the peasant girl, Olga, *"a great strapping wench"*.

K HAD TAKEN OLGA'S ARM AND WAS LEANING HIS WHOLE WEIGHT ON HER... IT WAS PLEASANT, WALKING WITH HER. K. STRUGGLED AGAINST THE FEELING OF COMFORT SHE GAVE HIM, BUT IT PERSISTED...

At the inn, K is informed by the landlord that all the rooms are *"reserved exclusively for gentlemen from the Castle"*, and that *"he must not go anywhere except in the bar"*.

113

THE BEER WAS DRAWN OFF BY A YOUNG, UNOBTRUSIVE GIRL CALLED FRIEDA, WITH FAIR HAIR, SAD EYES, AND HOLLOW CHEEKS, WITH A STRIKING LOOK OF CONSCIOUS SUPERIORITY. AS SOON AS HER EYE MET K'S IT SEEMED TO HIM THAT HER LOOK DECIDED SOMETHING ABOUT HIM...

Intrigued, K asks Frieda if she knows Klamm, a powerful official of the Castle.

HA HA HA...

I'M NOT LAUGHING... PHHH HA HA..

WHAT ARE *YOU* LAUGHING AT ??

OLGA IS VERY CHILDISH!

WOULD YOU LIKE TO *SEE* HERR KLAMM?

Frieda invites K to observe Klamm through a peephole in a nearby door. K sees a paunchy, middle-aged man sitting quietly at his desk.

115

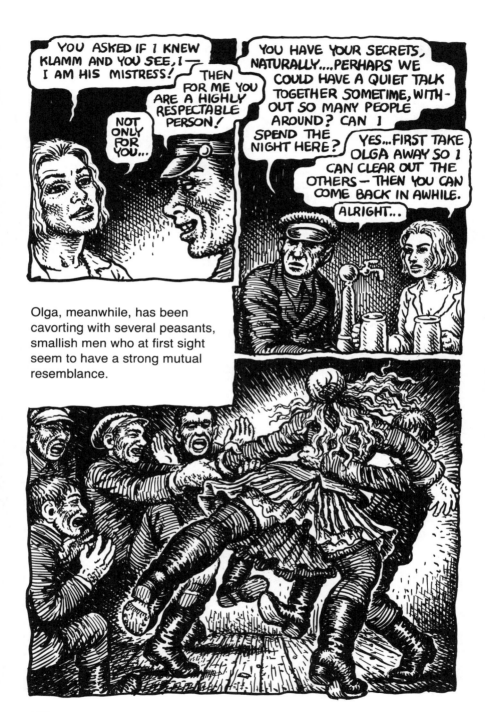

Olga, meanwhile, has been cavorting with several peasants, smallish men who at first sight seem to have a strong mutual resemblance.

117

"She drove them across the courtyard and into the stalls." K, hearing footsteps in the hallway, hides behind the counter.

"HE MUST HAVE GONE OUT LONG AGO," SAID FRIEDA COOLLY, PRESSING HER SMALL FOOT DOWN ON K'S CHEST...

...AND WHERE IS THE LAND SURVEYOR?

THE LAND SURVEYOR??

I FORGOT ALL ABOUT HIM...

MAYBE HE'S HIDDEN SOMEWHERE!

HE'D HARDLY HAVE THE NERVE TO DO THAT!

THERE WAS A CERTAIN HUMOR AND FREEDOM ABOUT HER WHICH K. HAD NOT PREVIOUSLY NOTICED.

PERHAPS HE'S HIDING UNDER HERE... NO, HE'S NOT HERE...

THE LANDLORD HAD SCARCELY LEFT THE ROOM BEFORE FRIEDA TURNED OUT THE ELECTRIC LIGHT AND WAS UNDER THE COUNTER WITH K.!

"MY DARLING! MY SWEET DARLING" SHE WHISPERED, NOT TOUCHING HIM, ONLY LYING ON HER BACK IN A LOVE-SWOON, HER ARMS OUTSTRETCHED, TIME SEEMINGLY ENDLESS IN THE FACE OF HER JOYOUS LOVE, SIGHING RATHER THAN SINGING A LITTLE SONG.

THEN, SEEING THAT K LAY LOST IN HIS THOUGHTS, SHE BEGAN TO TUG AT HIM LIKE A CHILD.

COME ON, ONE CAN'T *BREATHE* DOWN HERE!

THEY EMBRACED, HER LITTLE BODY BURNING IN K'S HANDS, IN A STATE OF UNCONSCIOUSNESS WHICH K TRIED AGAIN AND AGAIN BUT IN VAIN TO MASTER AS THEY ROLLED A LITTLE WAY, LANDING WITH A THUD AGAINST KLAMM'S DOOR, WHERE THEY LAY AMONG THE BEER SLOPS AND THE ACCUMULATED GARBAGE ON THE FLOOR...

HOURS WENT BY, HOURS IN WHICH THEY BREATHED IN UNISON, THEIR HEARTS BEATING TOGETHER, HOURS IN WHICH K. FELT HE WAS LOSING HIMSELF OR WANDERING INTO A STRANGE COUNTRY WHERE NO HUMAN BEING HAD EVER GONE BEFORE, A COUNTRY WHOSE VERY **AIR** WAS SO DIFFERENT FROM HIS NATIVE AIR THAT ONE COULD SUFFOCATE IN ITS STRANGENESS, AND YET SO ENTICING THAT ONE COULD ONLY GO FURTHER AND LOSE ONESELF IN IT.

This revelry is suddenly interrupted by *"a deep, authoritative, impersonal voice from Klamm's room,"* summoning Frieda. For K, this comes as a **relief** rather than a shock. He wakes Frieda, passing on the summons.

I'M WITH THE LAND SURVEYOR," SHE CALLED OUT, BEATING HER LITTLE FIST AGAINST KLAMM'S DOOR.

I'M NOT GOING... I'M NEVER GOING TO HIM AGAIN!

Frieda will become K's fiancée overnight and leave him the next day (taking up with one of the assistants!). But he will never lack female company, and the sub-erotic tension never abates. There is no *"sex"* in Kafka, in the overt sense of the word, but the psychological foreplay is infinite.

HIS EYES CAME TO REST ON AMALIA, HAVING TO LOOK UP TO HER, SHE BEING MUCH TALLER THAN HIM.

Olga will remain a constant companion, and K will immerse himself in the strange story of her sister, Amalia, whose refusal of the advances of a Castle official leads to the downfall of her family.

Advancing ever further into the labyrinth, K meets Pepi, Frieda's replacement as barmaid, who suddenly invites him to live with her and the chambermaids, Henriette and Emilie, in a small room at the bottom of the Herrenhof which is *"warm and cosy and tight"* and where the girls *"press together more tightly"*.

IT WILL MAKE THEM HAPPY TO HAVE A MAN AS HELPER AND PROTECTOR... IT MUST BE KEPT SECRET AND THIS SECRET WILL BIND US TOGETHER MORE CLOSELY THAN EVER ...

COME, OH PLEASE COME TO US!

HOW LONG IS IT UNTIL SPRING?

TILL SPRING? WINTER IS VERY LONG HERE, AND MONOTONOUS... BUT DOWN THERE WE DON'T WORRY ABOUT IT...WE'RE PROTECTED FROM WINTER...YES, ONE DAY SPRING COMES, AND SUMMER TOO, BUT THEY DON'T SEEM TO LAST MORE THAN TWO DAYS, AND EVEN ON THE MOST BEAUTIFUL DAY SNOW SOMETIMES FALLS....

K hardly has time to accept this unrefusable offer of a womb-room, when another of the novel's extraordinary women, the Landlady, enters to lead him in yet another direction of suppressed and fanciful eroticism.

YOU CAN'T *REMEMBER*?! THEN YOU'RE NOT ONLY *IMPUDENT*, BUT A *COWARD* AS WELL! YOU'VE NO BUSINESS TALKING ABOUT MY CLOTHES!

YESTERDAY YOU WERE IMPUDENT ENOUGH TO SAY SOMETHING ABOUT MY DRESS!

I CAN'T REMEMBER...

The Landlady now leads him to a small room, dominated by a huge wardrobe.

YOU DON'T EITHER... I SEE YOU ARE A LANDLADY, BUT YOU WEAR CLOTHES THAT ARE UNSUITABLE FOR A LANDLADY, AND THE LIKES OF WHICH NO ONE ELSE IN THE VILLAGE WEARS... THEY'RE OLD-FASHIONED, WORN OUT, AND NOT AT ALL SUITED TO YOUR AGE OR YOUR FIGURE OR YOUR POSITION!

WHAT *ARE* YOU, ACTUALLY??

A LAND SURVEYOR...

YOU'RE *LYING*! YOU NEVER TELL THE TRUTH!

!

The novel, as Kafka left it, ends with these words.

According to Max Brod there is a variant ending which finds K on his deathbed, when word comes from the Castle that he will be allowed to live and work in the village. There is endless critical speculation about a possible conclusion, or why Kafka never finished the novel. In fact, how could he have finished it?

Once having started out on this labyrinthine path, the Writer in him, as well as the Dying Man, most likely never intended finishing it, or, if he did, simply couldn't get there. What does it matter? Any *"ending"* would probably have spoiled this, one of the great literary *"journeys"* of our time.

K never gives up his quest to get to the Castle, although this gets further and further from him. If in **THE TRIAL** and **In the Penal Colony** the Law judged and punished, in **THE CASTLE** it is totally indifferent and non-manifest.

Kafka shores up figures from his own life, a schoolteacher, his boss, his father, of course, and casts them as impenetrable cogs in the Castle wheel. But K.-the-Night-Writer was mostly having fun, probably had no idea himself where the journey would lead him and, by August 1922, exhausted from real illness and unable to *"pick up the thread"*, he condemned K. to stay for ever in the village, elaborating his quest for acceptance, but in the end, like the Wandering Jew, unwelcome.

THE CASTLE, like Kafka's other novels, parades before the reader a seemingly limitless cast of "supporting" female roles, and repeats the central character's curious reliance on them. This is in no way a breath of feminism, for Kafka always sees these figures from a male point of view, making his traditional position quite clear early on. *"Women are traps which lie in wait for men everywhere, in order to drag them down into the Finite"*, he is reported to have said.

This natural disdain is of course a product of fear. Mature women especially frightened him, and his fascination for young girls lasted until the end of his life. He felt sorry for girls *"because of the transformation they have to go through to become women"*.

None of his female characters seems to have her own existence, but is spawned in his imagination in order to distract "K" or "Joseph K", to tempt and ensnare him. Kafka's sexual terror is put to the test time after time, yet these same women provide something more . . .

After nearly every scene in which the protagonist is made to find his way in the labyrinth — in the boarding house, at the Advocate's, at the Inn, at the court — one of these women is waiting for him with her own strange brand of "comfort". This is the role played by Olga and Pepi in **THE CASTLE**, and by the wife of the Court Usher in **THE TRIAL**.

The most blatant of these *"ensnaring"* women, and one who takes *"K"* further than most, is the character of Leni in **THE TRIAL**. She serves officially as *"nurse"* to the Advocate, but also seems to provide erotic distraction for all men accused by the Court, being especially aroused by those who display a sense of guilt . . .

SUDDENLY THERE WAS A NOISE FROM THE HALLWAY, LIKE THE SOUND OF CHINA SMASHING, AND EVERYONE STOPPED TO LISTEN.

I'LL GO SEE WHAT'S HAPPENED.

HARDLY HAD HE REACHED THE HALL OR HAD A CHANCE TO FIND HIS WAY IN THE DARK WHEN....

IT'S NOTHING, I ONLY THREW A PLATE AGAINST THE WALL TO BRING YOU OUT HERE.

I WAS THINKING ABOUT YOU, TOO!

ALL THE BETTER— COME ON...

THEY WALKED A FEW STEPS AND CAME TO A DOOR OF FROSTED GLASS...

GO IN...

IT WAS THE ADVOCATE'S STUDY, FITTED OUT WITH HEAVY PIECES OF OLD FURNITURE...

OVER HERE...

K LOOKED AROUND THE ROOM, WHICH WAS SO WIDE AND HIGH THAT THE ADVOCATE'S POOR CLIENTS MUST HAVE FELT LOST IN IT. HE IMAGINED HE COULD SEE THE LITTLE STEPS THESE VISITORS TOOK IN APPROACHING THE HUGE DESK.

130

K. DID NOT ANSWER, BUT MERELY TOOK LENI IN HIS ARMS AND PULLED HER TO HIM...

WHAT'S HIS RANK?

EXAMINING MAGISTRATE...

NOTHING BUT AN EXAMINING MAGISTRATE AGAIN...THE HIGHER OFFICIALS HIDE THEM-SELVES...YET HE'S SITTING ON A THRONE!

THAT'S ALL MADE UP...

IN FACT, HE'S SITTING ON A KITCHEN CHAIR WITH AN OLD HORSE-BLANKET THROWN OVER IT—BUT WHY DO YOU THINK ONLY ABOUT YOUR TRIAL?

ON THE CONTRARY, I DON'T THINK ABOUT IT ENOUGH...

DO YOU HAVE A GIRL-FRIEND?

K. TOOK OUT A PHOTOGRAPH OF ELSA...LENI STUDIED IT CLOSELY...

SHE'S LACED UP VERY TIGHT...I DON'T LIKE HER VERY MUCH...SHE'S COARSE AND CLUMSY... DOES SHE HAVE ANY PHYSICAL DEFECTS?

PHYSICAL DEFECTS??

YES, LIKE MINE... LOOK!

SHE SPREAD OPEN THE RING AND MIDDLE FINGERS OF HER RIGHT HAND. THE WEB OF SKIN WHICH JOINED THEM REACHED UP NEARLY AS FAR AS THE TOP JOINTS....

131

132

The outcome of these relationships is rarely "intimate" (Leni being an exception) and has more to do with power than personal feelings. Kafka's talent would mostly SUGGEST erotic encounter, rather than indulging his characters in that act which he found *"repellent and perfectly useless"*.

Yet, being Kafka, it is precisely this *"repulsive"* aspect of such an encounter which attracts him. Nowhere is he more clear about this than in a letter to Milena, describing the first sexual experience of his life with a young Prague shopgirl. This girl had apparently said or done *"something slightly obscene (not worth mentioning)"* in the hotel . . .

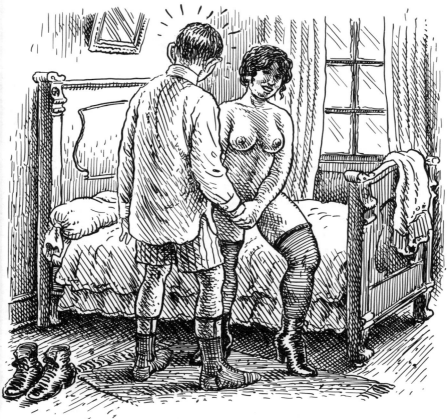

. . . And it was then he realized *"that disgust and dirt were a necessary part"* of the experience, that her *"one slight gesture, one small word"* were precisely what excited him.

"OTTLA LITERALLY CARRIES ME ON HER WINGS THROUGH THIS DIFFICULT WORLD."

In his personal life, women also provided a REFUGE from his father, the chief bearer of this Herculean task being his younger sister, Ottla.

135

She is the "other" woman in Kafka's life — perhaps the one who counted most and the one who represents the anti-face of the writer's "unclean" obsession. She was also his feminine physical counterpart, the photographs of them together showing an uncanny facial resemblance.

Ottla had always been his only comfort in the Kafka household and, in the early stage of his illness, he went to live with her at her farm in Zürau in northern Bohemia. Here, in his own words, they formed a *"marriage that is small and good, not with the usual violently contained current, but . . . a clear, straight-flowing current."*

For a while he even considered becoming a potato farmer . . .

. . . And, if that didn't work out there was always Palestine . . .

"I DREAMED OF GOING TO PALESTINE AS A FARMER OR ARTISAN... TO FIND A MEANINGFUL LIFE IN SECURITY AND BEAUTY... I LOVE THE SMELL OF PLANED WOOD, THE SINGING OF SAWS, THE BANGING OF HAMMERS... INTELLECTUAL WORK ALIENATES YOU FROM HUMAN SOCIETY."

The Promised Land would remain no more than a
dream for him. But, typically, he wrote that he
would at least be able to touch it with his finger on
a map.

Tuberculosis finally forced his retirement from his
insurance job in 1922, at the age of 39. For a while,
he returned under Ottla's wing, but for the most
part his illness was bleeding him to death internally.

Kafka was nonetheless to find a strange peace in the last months of his life. Whether he had actually changed, or at last had found a woman he could live with, he moved to Berlin in 1923 with 19-year-old Dora Diamant (1904-1952). Coming from an Orthodox Jewish family, she was independent enough to escape her ghetto background. Because of her, Kafka took a renewed interest in Judaism, and even briefly studied the Talmud.

Kafka seems to have seriously adapted to life with Dora, perhaps because he never had to create her in his own image — as he had done with Felice — or write letters to her: *"All the misery in my life was caused by letters . . ."*

Together the couple dreamed of moving to Tel Aviv, opening a Jewish restaurant where Dora would cook and Kafka — YES — wait on tables!

But in fact, Kafka's last months of peace were spent in utter poverty, in the eye of the approaching historical hurricane.

Berlin, 1923!

When he first came to Berlin, Kafka felt he had escaped from those phantoms which had forced him to write: *"They keep looking for me but, for the moment, they can't find me."* These were the same ghosts who *"drank kisses"* written in letters and who seemed to vampyrize his words and thoughts. Soon, he would ask Dora to burn many of his manuscripts. But the phantoms returned and forced him one night to write — appropriately — THE BURROW.

All this while, his tuberculosis was crawling up from the lungs into his larynx and, in his last months, he could only communicate by written notes, and could scarcely eat. In April, 1924, he was moved to a sanatorium near Vienna, but his condition continued to deteriorate until June.

Towards the end, he insisted that the doctor attending him give him morphine for the pain.

When Kafka regained consciousness for the last time, he apparently removed an icepack which had been placed on his neck, and threw it on the floor.

Three days later, in his obituary, Milena Jesenska called him *"a man condemned to regard the world with such blinding clarity that he found it unbearable and went to his death."*

In June, 1924, his "phantoms" saw to it — with their usual irony — that while dying of STARVATION, he would be correcting the galley-proofs of an astonishing masterwork called . . .

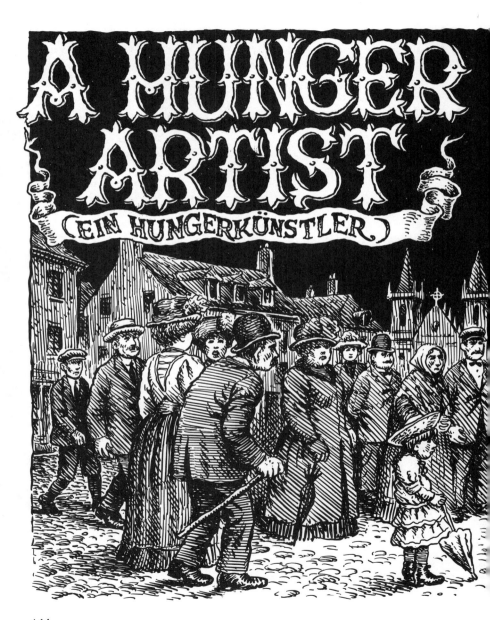

A HUNGER ARTIST

(EIN HUNGERKÜNSTLER.)

IN THE LAST FEW DECADES, THE INTEREST IN PROFESSIONAL HUNGER-ARTISTRY HAS GREATLY DIMINISHED. ONCE THE WHOLE TOWN CAME OUT TO SEE THE HUNGER-ARTIST. SOME EVEN BOUGHT SEASON TICKETS, AND AT NIGHT THE SCENE WAS BATHED IN THE LIGHT OF TORCHES.

GROUPS OF PROFESSIONAL WATCHERS, USUALLY BUTCHERS, WERE SENT TO WATCH HIM, IN CASE HE HAD SOME SECRET CACHE OF NOURISHMENT. BUT, DURING HIS FAST THE ARTISTE WOULD NEVER, EVEN UNDER COMPULSION, SWALLOW THE SMALLEST BIT OF FOOD; HIS PROFESSIONAL HONOR FORBADE IT. HE ALONE KNEW WHAT THE OTHERS DIDN'T: FASTING WAS THE EASIEST THING IN THE WORLD.

TICKETS

SEE THE HUNGER ARTIST

THE PERIOD OF FASTING WAS SET BY HIS IMPRESARIO AT FORTY DAYS MAXIMUM, BECAUSE AFTER THAT TIME THE PUBLIC BEGAN TO LOSE INTEREST. SO, ON THE FORTIETH DAY, WITH AN EXCITED CROWD FILLING THE ARENA AND A MILITARY BAND PLAYING, TWO YOUNG LADIES CAME TO LEAD THE HUNGER-ARTIST OUT OF HIS CAGE. WHEN THIS HAPPENED HE ALWAYS PUT UP SOME RESISTANCE...WHY STOP AFTER ONLY FORTY DAYS?!? WHY SHOULD THEY TAKE FROM HIM THE GLORY OF FASTING EVEN LONGER, OF SURPASSING EVEN HIMSELF TO REACH UNIMAGINABLE HEIGHTS, FOR HE SAW HIS ABILITY TO GO ON FASTING AS *UNLIMITED!*

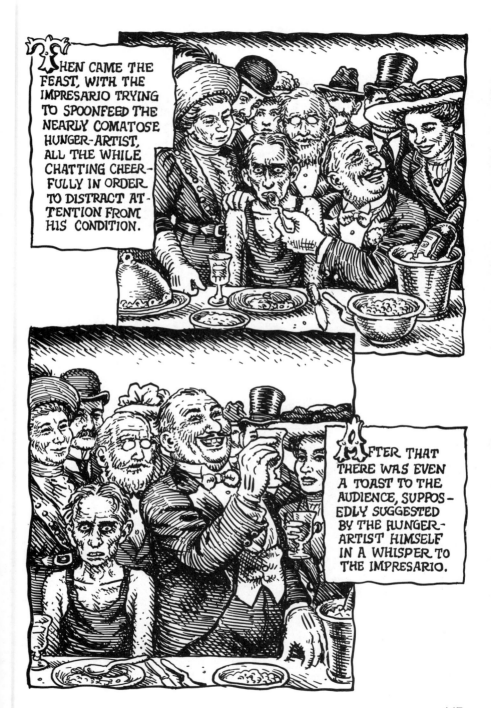

HEN CAME THE FEAST, WITH THE IMPRESARIO TRYING TO SPOONFEED THE NEARLY COMATOSE HUNGER-ARTIST, ALL THE WHILE CHATTING CHEERFULLY IN ORDER TO DISTRACT ATTENTION FROM HIS CONDITION.

FTER THAT THERE WAS EVEN A TOAST TO THE AUDIENCE, SUPPOSEDLY SUGGESTED BY THE HUNGER-ARTIST HIMSELF IN A WHISPER TO THE IMPRESARIO.

HE LIVED THIS WAY FOR MANY YEARS, HONORED BY ALL THE WORLD, YET TROUBLED IN HIS SOUL, DEEPLY FRUSTRATED THAT THEY WOULD NOT ALLOW HIS FASTING TO EXCEED FORTY DAYS. HE SPENT MOST OF HIS TIME IN A GLOOMY MOOD, AND WHEN SOME KIND-HEARTED PERSON WOULD TRY TO EXPLAIN THAT HIS DEPRESSION WAS THE RESULT OF THE FASTING, HE WOULD SOMETIMES FLY INTO A RAGE AND BEGIN RATTLING THE BARS OF HIS CAGE LIKE AN ANIMAL.

AS TIME WENT BY PEOPLE BECAME INTERESTED IN OTHER AMUSEMENTS, AND WERE REVOLTED BY PROFESSIONAL FASTING. THE HUNGER-ARTIST COULD NOT CHANGE JOBS, FANATICALLY DEVOTED TO FASTING AS HE WAS. SO, DISCHARGING THE IMPRESARIO, HE HIRED HIMSELF OUT TO A LARGE CIRCUS, WHERE HIS CAGE WAS PUT OUTSIDE, NEAR THOSE OF THE ANIMALS.

WORLD'S GREATEST HUNGER ARTIST

ASTOUNDING REVELATION OF HUMAN ENDURANCE

DO NOT ATTEMPT TO DETER HIM

NO FOOD IN 32 DAYS! HOW LONG CAN HE GO ON?

GAZE UPON THE MAN WHO DOES NOT EAT

DAZZLED THE SCIENTISTS PUZZLED THE PUBLIC

CHALLENGES ANYONE TO GO AS LONG AS HE WITHOUT EATING!

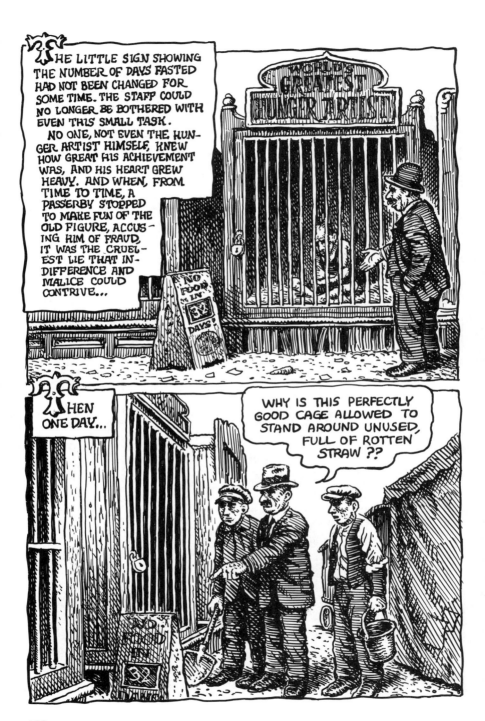

THE LITTLE SIGN SHOWING THE NUMBER OF DAYS FASTED HAD NOT BEEN CHANGED FOR SOME TIME. THE STAFF COULD NO LONGER BE BOTHERED WITH EVEN THIS SMALL TASK.

NO ONE, NOT EVEN THE HUNGER ARTIST HIMSELF, KNEW HOW GREAT HIS ACHIEVEMENT WAS, AND HIS HEART GREW HEAVY. AND WHEN, FROM TIME TO TIME, A PASSERBY STOPPED TO MAKE FUN OF THE OLD FIGURE, ACCUSING HIM OF FRAUD, IT WAS THE CRUELEST LIE THAT INDIFFERENCE AND MALICE COULD CONTRIVE...

WORLD'S GREATEST HUNGER ARTIST

NO FOOD IN 3X DAYS

THEN ONE DAY...

WHY IS THIS PERFECTLY GOOD CAGE ALLOWED TO STAND AROUND UNUSED, FULL OF ROTTEN STRAW??

BECAUSE...BECAUSE I COULD NEVER FIND ANY FOOD I LIKED... IF I *HAD* FOUND ANY, BELIEVE ME, I WOULDN'T HAVE MADE ALL THIS FUSS! I'D HAVE STUFFED MYSELF THE SAME AS YOU OR ANYBODY ELSE!

THESE WERE HIS LAST WORDS, BUT IN HIS BROKEN EYES ONE COULD SEE THE FIRM, IF NO LONGER PROUD, CONVICTION THAT HE WAS FASTING STILL....

ALRIGHT, CLEAN UP THIS MESS...

THEY BURIED THE HUNGER-ARTIST TOGETHER WITH THE STRAW. INTO HIS CAGE THEY NOW PUT A YOUNG PANTHER...

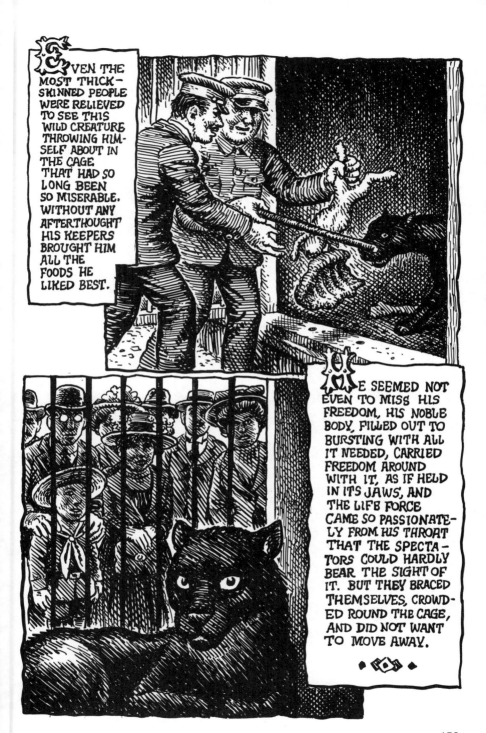

VEN THE MOST THICK-SKINNED PEOPLE WERE RELIEVED TO SEE THIS WILD CREATURE THROWING HIMSELF ABOUT IN THE CAGE THAT HAD SO LONG BEEN SO MISERABLE. WITHOUT ANY AFTERTHOUGHT HIS KEEPERS BROUGHT HIM ALL THE FOODS HE LIKED BEST.

E SEEMED NOT EVEN TO MISS HIS FREEDOM, HIS NOBLE BODY, FILLED OUT TO BURSTING WITH ALL IT NEEDED, CARRIED FREEDOM AROUND WITH IT, AS IF HELD IN ITS JAWS, AND THE LIFE FORCE CAME SO PASSIONATELY FROM HIS THROAT THAT THE SPECTATORS COULD HARDLY BEAR THE SIGHT OF IT. BUT THEY BRACED THEMSELVES, CROWDED ROUND THE CAGE, AND DID NOT WANT TO MOVE AWAY.

• ◈ •

153

AFTERWORD:

A Hunger Artist was one of the few stories Kafka exempted from his instructions to Max Brod that all his work, all his manuscripts and papers, be INCINERATED after his death. So, he was still trying to DISPOSE of himself; although, as the writer J-L Borges rightly points out: if he really wanted a bonfire, why didn't he just strike the match himself?

In any case, Brod, as we know, did not comply, and went on to edit what was, at that time, a confused jumble: chapters unnumbered or out of order, multiple versions, crossings-out, some works untitled (many of the titles we have were later provided by Brod).

A completely new edition is now being prepared by Kafka scholars in Germany, based on more accurate and up-to-date readings.

Manuscripts left in the hands of Dora Diamant were not so "lucky", being taken in a raid on her Berlin apartment in 1933. Ironically, Kafka's wish was most likely carried out by the book-burning Gestapo.

Milena Jesenska and Kafka's three sisters were deported to, and died in, concentration camps. Ottla cut off a possible escape route by divorcing her non-Jewish husband, so as not to separate herself from her family. Had Kafka lived, the Holocaust would surely have been his fate as well.

As for Kafka's Ghetto, Adolph Hitler had the idea of turning it into a kind of "memorial to an extinct race", after having extinguished that race himself, and the State Jewish Museum is, in a curious way, his legacy.

K himself was slowly becoming The ADJECTIVE, which would be known by many more people than would ever read his books. Of course — let's face it — this has not a little to do with the sound of his terrifiK name and its terrifiK GermaniK ''K''s, Kutting their way like Kutlasses through our Kollective Konsciousness.

(SEE PAGE 5)

EMBLEM OF JACKDAW ('KAVKA' IN CZECH) USED BY KAFKA'S FATHER AS A LETTERHEAD FOR HIS HABERDASHERY AND DRY-GOODS BUSINESS

(In his diary he wrote: ''I find the letter 'K' offensive, almost disgusting, but I still use it.'') Could he have become the powerful ADJECTIVE — ''KAFKAESQUE'' — if his name had been Schwarz or Grodzinski or Blumenthal?

The ADJECTIVE has come to stand for many things, not all of them having to do with Franz Kafka. He is often thought of as spooky, or as a writer of mysteries, or a kind of pre-Orwellian visionary mapping out the boundaries between bureaucracy and dictatorship. One recent film, which has the indecency to bear his name in the title, has him entering the Castle and finding a mad scientist performing lobotomies in the interest of mastering the world.

There is now a literary science called "Kafkalogy", and professors who vaunt themselves as "Kafkalogists". The literature ABOUT Kafka alone runs into thousands of volumes. A lot of it tells about his search for God and meaning in an Absurd universe, or the search for individuality in the Age of Bureaucracy. One American psychologist, ascribing every conceivable sexual fantasy to Kafka, including the wish to be sodomized by his father, interprets the Door of the Law in THE TRIAL as the unattainable entry to Mother Kafka's vaginal canal.

On the other hand, he has inspired some truly ecstatic and insightful prose, to be found in Ernst Pawel's **The Nightmare of Reason**; Elias Canetti's **Kafka's Other Trial**; and Pietro Citati's **Kafka**. Ritchie Robertson's **Kafka: Judaism, Politics and Literature** is a good source of information for Kafka's Jewish roots; and the French critic, Marthe Robert, has done some excellent work on the author's relationship to Prague.

Still, the first and best of all "Kafkalogists" is . . . Franz Kafka. Nearly everything that has been said or written about him can be found in his famous **Letter To His Father** (1919) where it is plain that nothing — but NOTHING — in his own life ever escaped his scrutiny.

In this extraordinary document he examines his childhood and adulthood under a microscope, urging his father to peer in with him. *"You asked me lately why I'm afraid of you,"* it begins, and is followed by a fifty-page *"answer"*.

By this time he had become, in his own words, *"a memory come alive"*, and his insight into his own past and neurosis is probably without equal in modern literature.

158

Kafka's diaries, kept between the years 1910-1923, and full of fragments of personal observation, do not begin to achieve the uncanny level of self-revelation found in the **Letter To His Father**. For this document is not simply a catalogue of horrors against a parent, summed up in adulthood behind the new-found bravery of a postage-stamp. Typically, in accusing his father, Kafka finds myriad excuses for damning himself as well.

It was impossible for him ever to take the offensive, for his instinct would immediately turn this into SELF-ABUSE . . .

If his father undid his braces and hung them over the back of a chair in preparation for a whipping, but then spared his son at the last moment, the boy felt himself to be in his debt. When Hermann Kafka treated his Czech employees like dirt, it was Franz who felt remorse on his behalf: *"even if I, meaningless creature that I was . . . had licked their feet, it would have been no compensation for the way that you, the master, had scolded them"*.

In summing up his life-long lack of self-confidence and boundless guilt with regard to his father, he recalls the last line of **THE TRIAL**, just as the knife is plunged into Josef K's throat: *"It was as if the shame of it should outlive him."*

Of course, Kafka was incapable of handing this *"letter"* over himself, so he left the task to his mother. On seeing the contents, she thought better of it and returned it to its sender, never to be delivered to its rightful recipient.

Kafka's relationship to his native Czechoslovakia was (and still is) ambiguous, to say the least. If Prague was the centre of his universe, the place where he was born and spent nearly all his life, it hardly ever figures in his works as itself. He NEVER names it or describes it in his fiction.

In one of the rare stories where he seemingly alludes to it, **The City Coat of Arms**, it is in the following terms: *"All legends and songs originating in this city are filled with nostalgia for a prophesied day when the city would be smashed to bits by five blows in rapid succession from a gigantic fist."*

Even in **THE TRIAL**, which ostensibly takes place against a background of (still unnamed) Prague, the dreariness of the surroundings hardly sings the praises of this famous capital. Its beautiful churches and public monuments seem as sombre as everything else described in the novel.

This purposeful omission, along with the fact that Kafka continued to write in German even after the creation of the Republic of Czechoslovakia in 1919, did not endear him to the Czechs. In the decade following his death, not one of his books was available to the public in his native country. And, even then, translations of his works in the Czech language were few and far between.

After the Second World War, under the Communist regime imposed by Moscow in 1948, Kafka became a thorn in the collective side. The influential Marxist critic, Georg Lukacs, had written of his *"aesthetically appealing, but decadent modernism"*, and his writings were clearly out of line with the obscure tenets of so-called *"socialist realism"*, which insisted on a photographic reproduction of reality as conceived under socialism, an artistic *"ism"* based more on political expediency than on actual content.

But perhaps the real danger in dissident Czechs reading Kafka is precisely that they took him for a REALIST. Those few who could get their hands on a smuggled-in copy of **THE TRIAL** found little there that differed from their daily lives in Stalinist Czechoslovakia with its informers, its public denunciations and especially its *"show-trials"* of ex-Communist leaders, accusing themselves publicly of crimes they never committed.

Since the IMMINENT TRIUMPH OF WORLD SOCIALISM ON THE SOVIET MODEL had already rendered the bourgeois Kafka obsolete, it was only logical to prohibit the distribution of his works.

In 1963, on the occasion of the 80th anniversary of his birth, a *"Kafka Congress"* was held at Liblice near Prague, ostensibly for the purpose of rehabilitating the writer. In his speech opening the conference, the distinguished critic Ernst Fischer declared: *"We have some catching-up to do. Kafka is a writer who concerns everybody."* This was followed by a number of papers re-establishing Kafka's place in European literature — in effect making him *"kosher"* for Czech Communists — pointing out that he was part of that movement in Prague German literature which fostered the humanist tradition and countered the rise of world imperialism.

This brief moment of glory did not outlive the *"Prague Spring"* of 1968 or its demise under the runners of Soviet tanks. Kafka's works were again banned, although his tombstone in Strasnice Jewish Cemetery was honoured, presumably as a tourist attraction.

In the *"free Prague"* of the 1990s, where his books are not banned (though not necessarily read) you can buy a Kafka TEE-SHIRT on every streetcorner in the tourist quarter, or his image on porcelain plates or artisanal wood carvings. You can take a *"Kafka"* tour (*"Have lunch with Kafka"* — no joke) and visit all the Prague landmarks where his ghost walks. Soon, like Mozart in Salzburg, you'll be able to eat his face on chocolate.

(A welcome antidote to this is the newly-founded Franz Kafka Society in the Old Town Square, which seriously seeks to revive Prague's Jewish heritage.)

This NEW PRAGUE with its burgeoning tourist culture out of the American mould, begins to look a bit like . . .

THE "NATURE" THEATRE OF OKLAHOMA

. . . Kafka's very own Czech version of the New World with its guiding principle of SOMETHING FOR EVERYBODY. This very special Old World fantasy of PROMISE and boundless good fortune forms the last fragmentary chapters of his unfinished novel **DER VERSCHOLLENE** (The Man Who Disappeared) — written between 1912 and 1913 — which Max Brod called **AMERIKA.**

Kafka planned to write a book showing *"New York at its most modern"*, so modern in fact that the bridge over the East River connects the city to Boston on the other side! What's more, on the very first page, the young hero Karl Rossman first sights the Statue of Liberty holding a *"sword"* (!) which was *"stretched up high, and round it blew the free winds of heaven."*

Rossman has been *"packed off to America by his parents because he had been seduced by a servant girl and had got her pregnant."* Very much like Kafka's shopgirl in the Prague hotel, this family maid seems to have done one of those things *"not worth mentioning"* to get him into her bed, accompanied by the usual mixture of yearning and loathing. We are given the news of this event in the very first sentence of the book, leaving no doubt that we are in Kafka territory, the central character being punished when he is not even at fault.

Why this punishment should be called *"America"* or why Rossman should be banished so far afield from his native Bohemia, is a matter of conjecture. But it gives Kafka, like so many European writers of his generation, a chance to fantasize about that mythical place he would never visit and to re-create it in his own special image.

Kafka claimed that his model for **AMERIKA** was **DAVID COPPERFIELD,** but Rossman is more of a latter-day Pinocchio, a wide-eyed exile trying to find his way in the demonic REAL WORLD, fair game for all conceivable hustlers and vultures.

On the ship in New York harbour, Karl is greeted by his Uncle Jakob, a self-made immigrant who is also a Senator and who becomes an authority figure somewhat on the scale of Hermann Kafka. Inevitably, in spite of himself, Rossman will prove disobedient to this, as well as other, parental figures in the novel.

Uncle Jakob introduces him to Mr. Pollunder, a
wealthy New Yorker who takes him for a ride in his
car, allowing Karl his first real look at a very curious
American landscape . . .

"...THE ROADS AND PAVEMENTS WERE CHOKED
WITH TRAFFIC WHICH CHANGED DIRECTION EVERY
SECOND, AS IF CAUGHT IN A WHIRLWIND OF NOISE,
DIVORCED FROM HUMANITY AND COMING FROM
SOME STRANGE ELEMENT... EVENTUALLY THEY
ARRIVED AT THE SUBURBS, WHERE MOUNTED
POLICE DIVERTED THEIR CAR INTO SIDE ROADS
DUE TO A DEMONSTRATION BY STRIKING METAL
WORKERS... AND WHEN THE CAR EMERGED
ONCE MORE FROM THE DARK BACK-STREETS AND
CROSSED A HUGE THOROUGHFARE, A PERSPECT-
IVE OF PAVEMENTS FANNED OUT BEFORE THEM,
FURTHER THAN THE EYE COULD SEE, FILLED
WITH MASSES OF PEOPLE MOVING WITH TINY
STEPS, WHOSE SINGING WAS MORE UNIFIED
THAN THE SOUND OF A SINGLE HUMAN VOICE..."

Taking Karl home with him, Pollunder introduces his daughter, Klara, the essence of a European boy's dream/nightmare image of the all-American girl.

I REALLY FEEL SORRY FOR YOU, YOU'RE A PASSABLY GOOD-LOOKING BOY...IF YOU'D LEARNED JU-JITSU YOU PROBABLY WOULD HAVE BEATEN ME!

After falling out with his uncle, Karl goes on the road and meets up with a duo of con-men, the Irishman Robinson and the Frenchman Delamarche, who proceed to bilk him of the few possessions he has left, including the Veronese salami his mother has packed for him.

Getting free of these tramps, Rossman is swept up by another of Kafka's "comforting" women, this time the Manageress of a hotel.

LISTEN, WOULDN'T YOU LIKE TO TAKE A JOB HERE IN THE HOTEL?

In the great tradition of such novels of ambitious young men in America, he becomes a lift-boy. But this is no ordinary job. In this particular hotel, there are no less than thirty lifts! Karl is forced to work twelve-hour shifts and take naps standing up. He tugs at the cables in order to bring his guests down faster, so as not to lose them to other lift-boys.

The lift-boys are lorded over by the Head Porter, a sadistic tyrant whose sole function is to punish them . . .

YOU HAVE TO GREET ME EVERY TIME YOU WALK BY ME, EVERY SINGLE TIME, WITHOUT EXCEPTION! WHEN YOU SPEAK TO ME, YOU HAVE TO STAND WITH YOUR CAP IN YOUR HAND! YOU ALWAYS HAVE TO SAY "SIR" TO ME AND NEVER "YOU!' AND YOU HAVE TO DO THIS EVERY TIME—EVERY SINGLE TIME !!

EVERY TIME?

When Karl commits a misdemeanour on duty, he is not merely fired by the Head Porter, but is also physically and verbally abused . . .

His only refuge is the house where Robinson and Delamarche are holing up with a grossly fat woman called Brunelda, a flat where Karl for a time becomes a virtual prisoner.

He is lost in the New World, friendless, penniless, homesick, until he comes upon a poster . . .

Answering the call, Rossman arrives and goes to one of the 200 reception desks! where new members are being recruited. When asked his name, he gives the nickname he had in his previous job . . .

In the "NATURE" THEATRE OF OKLAHOMA (the word "nature" supplied by Max Brod), the possibilities for employment of any and every kind are limitless, dancing girls dressed as angels play trumpets before huge banquet tables. If K. had finished the book, claims Brod, Rossman would have found again, through *"magic, his vocation, freedom and integrity, as well as his parents and his homeland."*

In any case, Karl is hired — as is everyone else —
and starts his train journey from the East to
Oklahoma, with Kafka again displaying his singular
European sense of American geography . . .

"ON THE FIRST DAY THEY TRAVELLED THROUGH A
HIGH MOUNTAIN RANGE...EVEN LEANING YOUR NECK OUT
OF THE WINDOW, YOU COULDN'T SEE THEIR PEAKS...WIDE
MOUNTAIN STREAMS APPEARED, ROLLING DOWN INTO THE
FOOTHILLS, THEN PLUNGING UNDER BRIDGES OVER WHICH
THE TRAIN ROARED; AND THEY WERE SO CLOSE THAT
THE COLD BREATH RISING OFF THEM CHILLED THE SKIN
OF YOUR FACE."

It was the fairy-tale version of America of a young Czech-born Jew who had never been further than the Italian lakes, an image which seems to be resurfacing in postcommunist Prague, a city trying to make up for years of lost dreams, repressed sexuality, and lack of communication with the outside world.

The fake American dream, in which no one has to deny himself anything, in which everything can be obtained by credit card has become, in some respects, a replacement for the fake "reality" imposed on the city in the past four decades.

The old town now has an American colony with its own daily newspapers, Chicago pizza parlours, tee-shirts *("Czech 'em out!")*, and a new Iron Curtainless breed of McDonald's-chomping Czechs, for whom such drivel must seem like *haute cuisine* after forty years of "socialist" nourishment.

It's the NATURE THEATRE OF PRAGUE — something for everyone — in which Kafka is finding his place amidst the KITSCH. After years of ignoring him or treating him as a pariah, the new Czech Republic is finally discovering its strange Jewish son, no longer a threat and suddenly BANKABLE as a tourist attraction. The irony would not have been lost on him.

ROBERT CRUMB is the creator of **Fritz the Cat, Mr Natural** and other legendary cartoon figures. He is one of the pioneers of American underground comics and his work has been celebrated at the Museum of Modern Art in New York.

DAVID ZANE MAIROWITZ is the author of **Wilhelm Reich for Beginners** and **The Radical Soap Opera.** His radio plays are regularly produced by the BBC and throughout Europe.

Note: All translations from the German by D.Z.M.